A KIND OF POWER
The Shakespeare-Dickens Analogy

MEMOIRS OF THE
AMERICAN PHILOSOPHICAL SOCIETY
Held at Philadelphia
For Promoting Useful Knowledge
Volume 105

A KIND OF POWER
The Shakespeare-Dickens Analogy

ALFRED B. HARBAGE

*Cabot Professor of English Emeritus,
Harvard University*

Jayne Lectures for 1974

AMERICAN PHILOSOPHICAL SOCIETY
INDEPENDENCE SQUARE · PHILADELPHIA
1975

The Jayne Lectures of the American Philosophical Society honor the memory of Henry La Barre Jayne, 1857-1920, a distinguished citizen of Philadelphia and an honored member of the Society. They perpetuate in this respect the aims of the American Society for the Extension of University Teaching, in which Mr. Jayne was deeply interested. When in 1946 this organization was dissolved, having in large measure fulfilled its immediate purposes, its funds were transferred to the American Philosophical Society, which agreed to use them "for the promotion of university teaching, including *inter alia* lectures, publications and research in the fields of science, literature, and the arts."

Accepting this responsibility, the Society initiated in 1961 a series of lectures to be given annually or biennially by outstanding scholars, scientists, and artists, and to be published in book form as *Memoirs* of the Society. The lectures are presented at various cultural institutions of Philadelphia. Thus far the following, including the series published in the present volume, have been presented:

February 21, 28, March 7, 14, 1961. Per Jacobssen. *The Market Economy in the World of Today.* University Museum, University of Pennsylvania. Memoirs, Vol. 55 (1961).

March 7, 14, 21, 1962. George Wells Beadle. *Genetics and Modern Biology.* University Museum, University of Pennsylvania. Memoirs, Vol. 57 (1963).

March 6, 13, 20, 1963. Doris Mary Stenton. *English Justice Between the Norman Conquest and the Great Charter, 1066-1215.* University Museum, University of Pennsylvania. Memoirs, Vol. 60 (1964).

March 10, 17, 24, 1964. Ellis Kirkham Waterhouse. *Three Decades of British Art: 1740-1770.* Philadelphia Museum of Art. Memoirs, Vol. 63 (1965).

May 3, 4, 6, 7, 1965. William A. Fowler. *Nuclear Astrophysics.* The Franklin Institute. Memoirs, Vol. 67 (1967).

February 14, 21, 28, March 7, 1966. Jacob Viner. *The Role of Providence in the Social Order: an Essay in Intellectual History.* University Museum, University of Pennsylvania. Memoirs, Vol. 90 (1972).

October 31, November 7, 14, 1967. Douglas Bush. *Pagan Myth and Christian Tradition in English Poetry: Three Phases.* Free Library of Philadelphia. Memoirs, Vol. 72 (1968).

April 4, 9, 11, 1968. Sir Peter Medawar. *Induction and Intuition in Scientific Thought.* University Museum, University of Pennsylvania. Memoirs, Vol. 75 (1969).

February 13, 18, 20, 1969. Robert H. Dicke. *Gravitation and the Universe.* The Franklin Institute. Memoirs, Vol. 78 (1970).

March 3, 6, 10, 1970. Gunnar Myrdal. *Critical Views of the United Nations.* University Museum, University of Pennsylvania.

March 5, 6, 7, 1974. Alfred B. Harbage. *A Kind of Power: The Shakespeare-Dickens Analogy.* Annenberg Center for Communication Arts and Sciences, University of Pennsylvania. Memoirs, Vol. 105 (1975).

Copyright © 1975 by The American Philosophical Society
Library of Congress Catalog Card Number
International Standard Book Number 0-87169-105-1

Contents

Foreword vii

Author's Preface ix

   I. Two are Chosen 1

  II. Art to Enchant 25

 III. The Welcome Message 51

Index 75

Foreword

When a scholar attains distinction in some field of studies to which he has devoted the major part of his effort he is naturally thought of as a specialist in that field—which he is. It is also often assumed—and this may or may not be true—that his interest is so focused on that field that he has no time to think of anything else in a scholarly way. He may even be branded as a "narrow" specialist, a designation which conveys a slight opprobrium.

That Alfred Harbage is a specialist is undeniable. No one who is familiar with the titles in almost any card catalog can fail to recognize it. Books like *Shakespeare's Audience, As They Liked It, Shakespeare and the Rival Tradition* proclaim him a Shakespearean. That he was chosen to be the general editor of the Pelican Shakespeare in the Penguin series and that he was invited to deliver the British Academy Shakespeare lecture a few years back confirms his reputation in the field. But that he is not a narrow specialist—with or without opprobrium—is apparent from his books on *Cavalier Drama, Thomas Killigrew,* and *Sir William Davenant,* to say nothing of his *Annals of English Drama*. True, his main interest has been the English drama from 1500 to 1700, and of course the emphasis has been on Shakespeare.

But few people are aware of his interest in the novel and that all his life he has had a second love, Charles Dickens. And so, when the committee on the Jayne lectures invited him to deliver the series that now appears in the present volume, and allowed him to choose the subject, it was not a great surprise to some of us that he chose to combine two of his lifelong interests. No narrow specialist could have written these lectures. One must be steeped in both men and their works. It is not a subject that one can "get up" for the occasion. A lifetime of reading and reflection is a prerequisite. This Alfred Harbage has brought to the task, and it is surprising how many things he has seen that the rest of us have not noticed. Of course, those who are familiar with some of his other books know how he can make interesting anything that he writes about. The lectures here published offered an exceptional occasion for him to bring his special gifts into full play. As a one-time colleague and longtime friend and admirer I take special pleasure in writing this brief foreword.

ALBERT C. BAUGH

Author's Preface

The Jayne Lectures of 1974 are here printed without alteration but with a small amount of illustrative material added in the documentary notes. In delivering the lectures I introduced the first and third with a few explanatory remarks, the substance of which follows.

After my topic was announced in a program of the American Philosophical Society in 1973, I was several times asked, in a friendly but quizzical way, whether I really believed Shakespeare and Dickens to be comparable, the second as great as the first. I explained that the question did not concern me. It was not my intention to place the two in competition, but to try the experiment of using each as touchstone of the other. I would dwell upon the similarities I seemed to detect in their lives and literary works, thus presenting an analogy and not a comparison.

Of course there are risks involved. Shakespeare's Fluellyn concludes that Monmouth County and Macedonia "is both alike" because "There is a river in Macedon and there is also moreover a river in Monmouth . . . and there is salmons in both." The defect in logic is of a kind not totally unknown in literary criticism, but it does not adhere inevitably to the analogical method; in fact Fluellyn's remark would be fairly rational if there actually were salmon in the streams of Macedonia and he were speaking to sports fishermen. The true limitation of analogy is that it is bound in some measure to be reductive. Valuable qualities in the works of one author *vis-à-vis* those of another may reside in *dissimilarity*. However, it has not been my ambition to produce a complete appraisal of the works of Shakespeare and Dickens, assuming that such could be done in three hours of discourse by a mortal of my frailty. I have been content to deal with appealing features of a relatively simple kind, such as tend to be increasingly slighted as literary investigations become increasingly subtle. There may be value in the suggestion that the power exercised by the works of these two great makers derives mainly, even though not exclusively, from qualities they possess in common.

Although analogies are necessarily reductive, they are less likely than comparisons to be invidious. The trouble with the process of comparison—treating differences as well as similarities—is that it forces us to speak in terms of superiority and inferiority. We cannot point to the superiority of an author, in this or that respect, without pointing to the inferiority of the one with whom he is being compared. We may discover, to our dismay, that we are conducting an exercise in counterdestruction. For instance, if we compare Shakespeare's treatment of Shylock with Dickens's treatment of Scrooge, the former forced to join a Christian community by judicial coercion, the latter persuaded by visions of such a community at its homely best, we may find that we are picturing Shakespeare as a barbarian compared with Dickens a civilized man. On the other hand, if we quote certain speeches in *The Merchant of Venice*—Shylock's on unchristianly Christians, Portia's on the quality of mercy, Lorenzo's on the music of the spheres "Still quiring to the young-eyed cherubins"—and then quote in comparison certain choric or gnomic passages in *A Christmas Carol*, we may seem to be demonstrating that Shakespeare wrote with a quill from an angel's wing, Dickens with a rusty spike.

What makes comparisons "odorous" (to use Dogberry's discriminating term) is their way of misleading us into viewing non-equivalents as equivalents. Dickens's literary art did not flower in an age of the *sententiae* and of verbal music, and hence did not distil itself in passages of matchless incisiveness or lyrical beauty. *His* mastery is displayed in prose passages of mixed narration and description of a kind not found in Shakespeare—such as those taking us into Scrooge's hole-in-the-wall counting house, where Cratchit tries to warm his hands at his candle while that hopeful boy in the outside sleet tries to sing a carol through the keyhole, his "scant young nose gnawed and mumbled by the hungry cold." To invoke even for a moment the idea of verbal ineptitude in connection with a writer who, with an unfailing air of spontaneity, can make us see things we can never forget is patently absurd. So far as comparing methods of Christian conversion is concerned, we need only remind ourselves that, while *A Christmas Carol* is truly a story of conversion, *The Merchant of Venice* just as truly is not. The latter is a story of a community drawing together in defense against a force deemed hostile to it. By a lamentable accident of history this force is represented in the person of a Jew.

If seen as wholes, works of art enhance each other when placed in juxtaposition. Dickens called his tale "a whimsical sort of masque." It would not be a bad term for *The Merchant of Venice*. Shakespeare was aware of the whimsicality of his picture of life in Venice and Belmont. We now fervently wish that he had made his moneylender a gentile, like Scrooge, but the fact remains that both Shylock and Scrooge are triumphs of serio-comic literary portraiture. The works in which they appear are imaginatively conceived, ingeniously constructed, wonderfully well written, and successful in providing in each case a few hours of exhilarating entertainment. How much more should we ask? If we raise the moral issue, as we must, the least we can say is that neither was designed in its time and place to do anyone any harm. Shakespeare and Dickens were both aware of the ambiguous nature of a mercantile-Christian community, English or "Venetian," and of the fact that the alienated figure is not solely responsible for his situation. But the overriding message of both was that it's good to be joined with others in friendship, love, and social amity, and not good to be morose, bitter, and alone.

Writers must be very great when works like these represent anything but the apex of their achievement. *A Christmas Carol* is one of those things, like one's front doorknob, which has become too familiar to be really seen. The clever Edwardians who dismissed Dickens as one who had infatuated them in childhood, always with the prideful air that they had now put aside childish things, were generalizing from their experience with the *Carol, Oliver Twist,* and *The Old Curiosity Shop*. We may doubt that they had been quite so familiar in childhood with *Bleak House, Little Dorrit,* and *Great Expectations,* or indeed ever became so. Whether or not it has delighted us in childhood, or bored us in an endless series of radio and television adaptations since, the *Carol* still remains a masterpiece. If we bring to the reading of Dickens the kind of high expectation and attentiveness we bring to the reading of Shakespeare, we find that he does not disappoint us. Perhaps if we could bring to the reading of Shakespeare a little more of the relaxation of attitude we bring to the reading of Dickens, and refrained from bringing his every line for judgment to every cultural, mythological, ethical, aesthetic high court, he too might be the gainer. At the beginning of my first lecture I indulge, no doubt unwisely, in a bit of irony, but it is directed not at Shakespeare but at those who revere him for the wrong reasons. I have tried hard in my analogy never to say anything about either of these writers which would reflect unfavorably upon the other.

I have not touched upon the subject of

Shakespeare's direct influence upon Dickens. The novelist knew the playwright early in life and knew him very well. However, I am inclined to believe that the character of his works would be much as it is if he had not known Shakespeare at all. If we are looking for Dickens's "models," we are obviously more likely to find them in works like *The Vicar of Wakefield* than in *As You Like It*. This does not mean that the influence of Shakespeare was negligible. Besides nourishing his natural dramatic bent, the plays had a pervasive influence upon his diction. In every one of his novels and with increasing frequency as his style matured, we come upon words and turns of phrase which would not be there were it not for his familiarity with Shakespeare. Also omitted from my discussion is the related topic of conscious discipleship and emulation. Probably Dickens never looked at any literary bow without wondering secretly whether he might not be able to bend it, but he seems to have recognized sensibly that he had small talent for writing verse. There could, however, appear on the nineteenth-century scene a Shakespeare of novelists, and Dickens came soon to know that hopeful glances were bent in his direction. His way of coping with this psychological burden was to indulge in occasional flippancy in his allusions to the Bard and in habitual self-mockery. He proclaimed himself "The Inimitable."

Since I have never taught Dickens or previously written about him, I publish these lectures in some trepidation. In a recent review in the *London Times Literary Supplement* another teacher and I were referred to as "senior card-carrying members of the Shakespeare Establishment." Although there was no intention to be offensive, I did not find the metaphor pleasing. I have never considered myself or anyone else a Shakespearean "authority," or association with him as a prerogative as distinct from a privilege. But it is true that I taught Shakespeare for a long time, and never without re-reading the play I was talking about, and that I "kept up" to the limit of my strength with Shakespearean commentary. Consequently, in writing about Shakespeare, (and I have never been reticent about doing so) I feel reasonably sure that my errors will not be of an elementary kind. I have no similar feeling of security in writing about Dickens although he has been my favorite novelist for a lifetime. I trust that those whom I shall refrain from calling "card-carrying members of the Dickens Establishment" will view me not as an intruder in their domain but as a respectful if awkward visitor. One of the awkwardnesses of which I am conscious is that I have not used for reference the "standard" text of the *Nonesuch Dickens,* the reason being that I have had only limited access to it while working on my topic. I have reread all of Dickens while preparing these lectures, and done so in the edition I own, published in forty-four volumes in 1890 by Estes and Lauriat of Boston. The edition of Shakespeare cited is the one-volume *Pelican,* 1969, of which I served as General Editor. To reduce the number of documentary notes, I have, whenever the identity of a work is clearly indicated in my discussion, inserted the reference in my text—the act and scene number for a play by Shakespeare, and the volume and chapter number, or the latter alone, for a novel, short story, or essay collection by Dickens.

Shakespeare and Dickens have enriched my life as they have the lives of so many others, and these lectures are my thank-you letter. I wish to express my gratitude also to two senior gentlemen and scholars, George W. Corner and Albert C. Baugh, who had the most to do with my being invited to give the lectures.

A. H.

Cherry Hill, N.J.
March, 1974.

A KIND OF POWER
The Shakespeare-Dickens Analogy

I. Two Are Chosen

1

WHEN Dickens arrived in Boston on his first visit to America, he was only twenty-nine, and he had not yet written the books which are now considered his best. However, he had already created Mr. Pickwick and Sam Weller, Dick Swiveller and the Marchioness, Little Nell, Oliver, and Smike; and these amiable waifs and eccentrics had warmed American hearts even where hearts were thought to be frostiest. The young writer was so lionized in New England, even by the president and faculty of Harvard, that a few firm voices declared the proceedings unseemly. Mrs. Andrew Norton, mother of Charles Eliot Norton, gave it as her view that the novels of Dickens were "well, some of them *very well*"; that is, in ruder words, that they ranged from fair to fairly good. Cornelius Felton, professor of Greek at the university, reported the remark to a friend, and also his brave reply: So far as the novels being *very well* was concerned, he "had been convinced since the first number of Pickwick, that one of the greatest minds of the age was coming out," and he "now entertained a profound conviction that Dickens was the most original and inventive genius since Shakespeare!" Having uttered the sacred name, the professor wavered in his profound conviction: "What do you say to that? Am I not more than half right?"[1]

We can understand his nervousness. To link Dickens's name with Shakespeare's might be consi-

---

[1] Letter from Cornelius C. Felton to Henry B. Cleveland, Jan. 24, 1842, quoted by E. Wagenknecht, *The Dickensian* 52 (1955): p. 10.

dered profane, or at least a social gaffe. When Shakespeare repined about his vocation (Sonnet III),

> . . . my nature is subdued
> To what it works in, like the dyer's hand,

he did not know how grandly the dye would fix—how in the eye of posterity his image, framed in a bloom of banners and escutcheons, would be tinted with noble hues: the patrician hauteur of Brutus, the princely sensibility of Hamlet, the right royal *élan* of Hal, the ducal grace of Prospero. How could his art be anything else but high? Alas, poor Dickens! Not one of his heroes stabs an emperor, spreads carnage with a bright rapier, leaves in rubble the villages of France, or keeps a musical sprite in thrall. Instead, if the metaphor may be shifted to the olfactory, there clings to his garments the scent of London slums, Tom-all-Alone's and Jacob's Island, of damp horse-blankets, kidneys stewing over coals, and, most nauseous of all to the fastidious, the whiff of all those nursing babies and grubby urchins tumbling about in his pages. How could his art be anything but low? Some readers who have found Shakespeare very hard going compared to Dickens have still preferred him, on the principle stated by the genteel youth whom Copperfield met at a dinner party, that it is better to be knocked down by an aristocrat than picked up by a plebeian.

Felton was speaking in 1842. He would have taken comfort could he have known that he was not the first and was not to be the last to link the names of Shakespeare and Dickens. Landor, Mitford, Lord Jeffrey, and others had already done so, while critics as various as Masson, Gissing, Chesterton, and Shaw were to be equally daring in times to come. Only during the brief winter of Dickens's reputation, severest in the nineteen-twenties, has this analogy met total scorn, when clever writers like Aldous Huxley were describing his characters as vulgarly infantile, and the Bloomsbury fellowship was finding his *gemütlich* art an occasion for gay mockery. Virginia Woolf's remark that, although she would gladly have been Shakespeare's cat, she would not "cross the road" to dine with Dickens[2] is of a kind which critics now thank God they never made. In the early nineteen-forties, just a century after Felton risked his respectability, Dickens emerged as the "Shakespeare of novelists," not only among the specialists in his work but among eminent arbiters of taste, the Lord Jeffreys of our day.

Lately I have been reading for the first time the Dickens critics extensively, and have been impressed by how good they are. Like Shakespeare he has had his Rymers and Voltaires, bright men but with minds too legalistic or compartmentalized, and he has also had the opposite, critics with minds apparently in a state of total flux, but it would be pointless to linger with them. Long before his death, able critics were aware of the nature of Dickens's achievement. Able ones since have submitted it to close analysis. They have cut through many snobberies and false assumptions, not only of the kind I have been suggesting but others as well, for instance the notion that a Victorian imagination must needs be inferior to an Elizabethan imagination, a novelist inferior to a dramatist, a writer in prose inferior to a writer in verse, and so on. In affirming that Dickens is a poet, his recent critics have returned to a principle which was current from classical times through the Renaissance. "I speak to show," said Philip Sidney, "that it is not rhyming and versing that maketh a poet." If Shakespeare could have read Dickens, he would have been astonished to learn that this poet had ever been considered anything else.

---

[2]"Correspondence," *The Nation*, Sept. 12, 1925.

From my praise of these critics I must make one small deduction. In comparing Dickens and Shakespeare, they are insufficiently specific. True, it is in the nature of genius that its products be unique—it is hard to associate the Incomparable and the Inimitable in other than a general way—but I seem to detect other reasons for the elusive nature of the discussion. Sometimes it appears that the critics are still timorous. If they particularize about similarities, they may expose themselves to ridicule by the defenders of Shakespeare's rights, even to the charge that they are *dragging him down* to Dickens's (or their own) level. Occasionally they seem aware of a different kind of hazard. Stressing the similarity in the moral attitudes of these two writers may serve only to fix both of them more firmly in the past, making them seem equally obsolete. I shall return to this point in my third lecture. What I wish to do in this one is to treat certain biographical and historical phenomena. Parallels in the personal careers of Shakespeare and Dickens (social, domestic, educational, professional) and in the careers of their written works (at home and abroad, and among critics and general readers) make the assumption of some degree of similarity in those works not only rational but almost inevitable.

2

We must recognize that, in most ways for most people, the England into which Dickens was born was so much more like the England into which Shakespeare was born than like the England of today that we can almost say that they came into the world as contemporaries. In families like theirs this holds true even of the life of the mind, but I am now speaking of material conditions, those things which immediately touched daily life. In 1812 just as in 1564 the rank and file experienced the same exclusion from the political and economic power structure, the same sanitary (or insanitary) living conditions, with a brief average lifespan and an especially high mortality rate among children; the same long working day at subsistence wages, with an unchanged Poor Law administered by parish officers; the same means of transportation (leg-power since few could afford horse-power, which was the only alternative); the same household facilities, with food cooked in an open fireplace; and so on. Most important, there was, in both 1564 and 1812, a gulf between the masses and the classes which could be crossed only by the highly gifted and enterprising. The bulk of the population performed unskilled or semi-skilled work with their hands, and were barely literate when literate at all. Their social superiors, except for the nobility, were so subtly graded that only an expert and an Englishman could tell when a man might legitimately call himself a gentleman.

Shakespeare and Dickens called themselves gentlemen, but each, like the shepherd's son in *The Winter's Tale (5, 2)*, was a "gentleman born" before his father. In *Oliver Twist (1, 5)* the charity boy Noah Claypole lords it over the foundling Oliver because he could "trace his genealogy all the way back to his parents." Dickens could trace his back to his grandparents. If he could do more, it is more than his biographers have been able to do with certainty, and the same is true of Shakespeare. Grandfather Richard Shakespeare was a tenant farmer of Snitterfield, and grandfather William Dickens was a steward at Crewe Hall. Since a tenant farmer is more than a farm laborer, and a steward more than a groom, we may see in these dim figures a sign that the great social gulf was about to be crossed. The crossing was made by the fathers of our two writers, John Shakespeare who became a tradesman and

John Dickens who became a clerk. Both were helped in making the crossing by marrying wives whose parents had already made it. The immediate families of both William and Charles were what we now call upwardly mobile, but their lower-middleclass standing was still recent and precarious.

We should not be surprised that nothing visible in their ancestry explains why they became great writers. In this as in everything else the beginning is mystery. At some time in some way certain appropriate genes had become auspiciously precoded—that is as much as we can say. It is hard to believe that these genes nestled among others transmitting signs of social inferiority. When the first families of Boston entertained Dickens, they delighted in his intelligence, good humor, and vitality, expecially in what they described as the "light" in his face, but they did not think he looked like a gentleman. This was not simply because of his crimson waistcoat, which should have been black, his free-flowing locks, which should have been shorter, or even what Longfellow described as the "slight dash of Dick Swiveller" in his manners. Tom Appleton said that, if the genius were removed from his face, he would look just like a cockney, and young Richard Dana that he had "stubby fingers, and a hand by no means patrician."[3] But in the Maclise portrait painted three years earlier Dickens looks almost alarmingly patrician, so we must reckon with the eye of the beholder. One wonders about Shakespeare. In the Droeshout engraving of the Folio he looks reassuringly patrician, but the Stratford bust, probably the better likeness, has been said by one discontented observer to resemble a "self-satisfied pork-butcher."[4] One must re-

---

[3]Edward F. Payne, *Dickens Days in Boston* (Boston, 1927), p. 43. Charles Francis Adams, *Richard Henry Dana* (2v., Boston, 1890) 1: pp. 31-32.

[4]John Dover Wilson, *The Essential Shakespeare* (Cambridge Univ. Press, 1932), p. 6.

coil at the idea that Shakespeare's poetry (at least the sonnets and tragedies) was set down with "stubby fingers."

Let me proceed with my unvarnished tale. John Forster, friend and biographer of Dickens, speaks of the home of one's early childhood as "the first warm nest of love."[5] Perhaps only a Victorian would dare use such terms, but truly the pre-adolescent years of both Shakespeare and Dickens were warm years. Each was an eldest son, and each—here things become almost uncanny—had two sisters and three brothers who survived infancy. When William was four, his father, although possibly illiterate, was given a term as chief administrative officer of the borough of Stratford. When Charles was five, his father, who was a clerk in the navy pay-office, was elevated to a post in Chatham, where he thought he could afford to rent an elegant house and employ two domestic servants. A boy in either family could feel that he belonged to a going as well as growing concern. Charles's father, immortalized in one of his aspects as Mr. Micawber, was popular, buoyant, and anxious to appear genteel. The signs are that William's father was much the same. Both overextended themselves and fell into debt. When Charles was twelve, his family was living in debtors' prison, and for four dreary months he himself was sitting with common "working boys" fixing labels to packets in a blacking warehouse. William's tumble from the "first warm nest of love" may have been less precipitous, but when he was twelve, his father, the ex-bailiff, ceased attending council meetings and was soon getting from his fellow-aldermen relief from assessments, as a man in financial straits. Nicholas Rowe, Shakespeare's first biographer, says (*Works,* 1709) that

---

[5]John Forster, *The Life of Charles Dickens* [1872-1874], ed. J. W. T. Ley (London, 1928), p. 554.

his father was forced to withdraw him from school because of "the narrowness of his circumstances, and the want of his assistance at home." If William was set to scraping kidskins in the glove shop on Henley Street, we can be sure he liked it no better than Charles liked packaging boot-polish.

The traumatic effects of Dickens's experience as a child laborer have perhaps been exaggerated because of the vividness with which he recorded his anguish. Many people have worn the scars of a first experience in earning their keep. Still, we must concede the probability of a special significance in his and Shakespeare's experience. Both would have known that literacy was their likeliest causeway over the bog of lifetime drudgery in shop, barnyard, or scullery, and that they were especially endowed as literates. Rowe's account of William's interrupted education is in accord with Jonson's testimony that he had "small Latin and less Greek." Neither of these writers attended a university and neither had enough preparatory schooling to be admitted to one. Both had schooling, probably good up to a point. One of Dickens's masters was an Oxford graduate, as was each master of the Stratford grammar school, but his formal education, interrupted several times before, ended completely when he was fifteen. If Jonson was right about his "small Latin," Shakespeare's must have ended earlier. Still both had been introduced into the world of letters to which they naturally belonged, and both had every incentive to cultivate on their own, and never to let lodge useless, "that one talent which is death to hide."

If John Shakespeare as well as John Dickens resembled Mr. Micawber in trusting that something would turn up, both of course were justified. What turned up was William and Charles, who created among other things family solvency. More significant than their similar kind of social and familial background is their adult behavior in respect to it. Both married, had children, and entered literate crafts which served as launching sites for careers in creative writing. In theory, the actor-playwright of London and the journalist-novelist of London should have been alienated—self-severed from their plain and in some respects humiliating backgrounds. In fact, neither of them was. Certainly Dickens was disinclined to dwell on the fact that his grandfather had been a groom risen to steward, his father a debtor in the Marshalsea, and himself a working boy. When asked by the editor of a biographical dictionary to supply information about his family, education, and so on, he did not actually falsify the facts but he did give them a genteel sheen.[6] Shakespeare probably was equally reticent about his Uncle Henry of Snitterfield, who was fined for not wearing a cap to church and for failing to pay for the team of oxen with which he had failed to mend the queen's highways. Nevertheless, the record is clear that neither of these men detached himself, in either an emotional or practical way, from his own people and place. The typical Elizabethan playwright was as alienated as the most demanding modern critic could wish. Shakespeare is the exception. He is the only one of them I know of who was buried in the church where he was baptized. He was predeceased by his parents and all his siblings but one. Those who dart off on the false trail of the "second best bed" should notice that his will provides for his sister Joan as well as his immediate family. Dickens wished to be buried near the scene of his Chatham childhood, but the will of the nation prescribed Westminster Abbey. He too was survived by one sister, but he did not have to provide for her in his

---

[6]Letter to J. H. Kuenzel, 1838, *The Letters of Charles Dickens*, ed. Madeline House & Graham Storey, 1 (Oxford, 1965): pp. 423-424.

will because he had already insured her welfare. The way he supported his father, mother, brothers, sisters, grown children, and even his relations-in-law is a tale of heroism. At twenty-six, when he was beginning to earn substantially, he wrote Forster, to whom he told things he told no one else, that he had just "paid fifty seven pounds, two and six pence for Edward Barrow," his mother's brother. "And so it always is," he said, "directly I build up a hundred pounds, one of my dear relations comes and knocks it down again."[7]

In spite of those "dear" relations, Dickens succeeded in building up far more than a hundred pounds. So also did Shakespeare. Both realized the dreams of their fathers by consolidating their middle-class family status. Recruits to the lower middle class, tradesmen and petty clerks, have not been favorite people with the British wellborn, who seem to feel that in ceasing to perform menial tasks they have lost the right to affection without gaining the right to respect. However, they themselves and their offspring do not share this view. Shakespeare on his way to school passed New Place, the town mansion of Stratford. In middle age he bought it, and he spent his last years there. Dickens in his walks with his father passed Gad's Hill, a mansion on the road from Rochester to Gravesend. In middle age he bought it, and he spent his last years there. Both now had income from investment, Shakespeare's naturally in land, Dickens's naturally in capital shares. Both boasted coats of arms, Shakespeare's bought from the Herald's Office, Dickens's simply appropriated. All this must be regarded less as social-climbing then as social digging-in. Dickens received with studied coolness the homage of lords and heads of state, and wanted no titles of honor. Forster said that "He would take as much pains to keep out of the

---
[7] Nov. 15, 1838, *Letters*, ed. House & Storey, 1: p. 454.

houses of the great as others take to get into them,"⁸ and intimated why. He was too proud to defer to those who were only technically his superiors. Something of this kind of sentiment must be imagined in all greatly gifted men, including Shakespeare. Although his biographers have made him the chum of one earl after another, there is no evidence that Shakespeare ever mingled socially with lords, or wanted to. His two dedicatory epistles to Southampton were written early in his career when the theaters were closed by the plague, and they should be interpreted in the light of the fact that he never wrote any more like them during his twenty-two remaining years.⁹ In this, too, he was ex-

---

⁸*Life*, ed. Ley, p. 635.

⁹The reader may be amused by a possible coincidence. In 1593 Lord Southampton received *Venus and Adonis* with the following epistle:

"I know not how I shall offend in dedicating my unpolished lines to your Lordship, nor how the world will censure me for choosing so strong a prop for so weak a burden; only, if your Honor seem but pleased, I account myself highly praised, and vow to take advantage of all idle hours, till I have honored you with some graver labor. But if the first heir of my invention prove deformed, I shall be sorry it had so noble a godfather, and never after ear so barren a land, for fear it shall yield me still so bad a harvest. I leave it to your honorable survey, and your Honor to your heart's content; which I wish will always answer to your own wish and the world's hopeful expectation.

Your Honor's in all duty,
William Shakespeare.

In 1836 Lord Stanley received a copy of *Sketches by Boz* with a letter apologizing for,

". . . the liberty I take in entreating your Lordship's acceptance of the accompanying volumes—the first I ever published. . . . The wish of Authors to place their works in the hands of those, the eminence of whose public stations, is only to be exceeded by the lustre of their individual talents, is, and always has been, so generally felt, even by the greatest Men who have ever adorned the Literature of this Country, that I hope it may be pardoned when it displays itself in so young, and so humble a candidate for public favor, as

My Lord
Your Lordship's most obedient
Humble Servant
Charles Dickens."

Fortunately we have more than scraps of documentary material on Dickens, and hence no elaborate theories have been based on this letter, which would have made him blush if he could have read it a few years later. (It appears in its entirety in *Letters*, ed. House & Storey, 1: pp. 126-27.) When claims began to appear that Shakespeare's works were not only inspired but actually written by a lord (Verulam was the first), the comic possibilities were seen in respect to Dickens. Imitating the penchant of the anti-Stratfordians for picking the least likely candi-

ceptional. In an era of dedicating poets, he was not a dedicating poet, and he alone among writers with his opportunities wrote no panegyrics for magnates, no masques for the Court, no private entertainments for noble households. One can easily imagine his watching the Globe filling up and subscribing to the kind of sentiment expressed by Dickens in a speech on low-priced literature:

> From the shame of the purchased dedication, from the scurrilous and dirty work of Grub Street, from the dependent seat on sufferance at my Lord Duke's table today, and from the sponging house and Marshalsea tomorrow . . . . from all such evils the people have set literature free.[10]

3

Of all the similarities in the situation of our chosen two, the most interesting is the professional. Each adapted his talents to a literary form old in its traditions but new in its accommodation to a popular audience massive enough to change the rules of the game of patronage. In Shakespeare's time there had been drama in England since the Middle Ages, and commercialized play-acting for over a century, but it was only a decade or two before he himself began to write that the theatrical industry had so organized itself as to serve a large, heterogeneous, urban clientele, voluntarily spending time and money on plays and thus helping to shape them. In the fifteen-seventies there appeared in London resident companies of adult actors performing in buildings especially designed for them, with auditoriums large enough and admission prices low enough to accommodate thousands. The actors

---

date, Andrew Lang nominated Herbert Spencer as the true author, and a writer in *Cornhill Magazine* made a case for Gladstone. See George H. Ford, *Dickens and His Readers* (Princeton, 1955), p. 163.

[10]Delivered in Birmingham, Jan. 6, 1853, *The Speeches of Charles Dickens*, ed. R. J. Fielding (Oxford, 1960), p. 157.

may be thought of as oral publishers, and Shakespeare, since he was a member of an acting company, as an author in partnership with his publishers, sharing their continuing interest in the size of audiences. In Dickens's time there had been printed prose fiction since the Renaissance, and for over a century the novel had been a conspicuous item in the Stationers' lists, but the library of Lydia Languish, while it may have been trashy, was far from cheap. Down to and including the time of Sir Walter Scott only the well-to-do could afford to buy novels. The change came during the early years of Dickens. The steam press, machine-made paper, and substitutes for leather binding brought down the costs of publishing; and the issuing of fiction in monthly parts, with *Pickwick Papers* as the first notable example, allowed thousands to buy novels who had never bought them before. Again a large and heterogeneous audience was being created, with a particular writer an important agent in its creation. Dickens, too, was in effect in partnership with his publishers (soon insisting on his seniority), with the same continuing interest as Shakespeare's in the number of paying customers.

Each interpreted his role in the same way. He was a professional entertainer, his primary object to please as many as possible and displease as few. In the second chorus in *Henry the Fifth* Shakespeare says, "We'll not offend one stomach with our play." Dickens's stated intention from the beginning was to avoid offense. In a late preface to *Oliver Twist* he uses the ten-letter word "prostitute," but it does not appear in the text of the novel itself, and the profession of the painted, gin-drinking Nancy remains a matter of inference. The difference between his picture of Fagin's stable of derelict boys and what its depravity would actually have been has been recognized as one of the wonders of the book. Of the picture of Wackford Squeers and Dotheboys Hall in *Nicholas Nickleby,* Dickens says that, far from exaggerating the brutalities of the Yorkshire farm-out schools, "I have kept down the strong truth and thrown as much comicality over it as I could, rather than disgust and weary the reader with its fouler aspects. . . ."[11] When his *Christmas Carol* was dramatized and the producer wanted to put steel braces on Tiny Tim, he said, ". . . this won't do! Remember how painful it would be to many of the audience having crippled children."[12]

In the first of his books on Dickens, Gissing treats the issue raised by this kind of deference to public taste. He cites Dickens's inquiry whether such and such a thing might be done in his current novel "without making people angry," and how enraged modern authors become at the idea that an artist should "stay his his hand until he has made grave inquiry whether Messers Mudie's subscribers will approve" and write "in homely fear of Mrs. Grundy!" This in 1898. Gissing states the ideal which has become more and more dominant among aspiring authors since: so far as ignoring public sentiment is concerned, "it is only when one does so that one's work has a chance of being good." Then he adds, "Dickens had before him no such artistic ideal; he never desired freedom to offend his public. Sympathy with his readers was to him the very breath of life; the more complete that sympathy the better did he esteem his work."[13] Gissing returned to the subject in a later essay: Dickens never wavered from "his prime purpose of sending forth fiction acceptable to the multitude."[14]

---
[11] To Mrs. S. C. Hall, Dec. 29, 1838, *Letters,* ed. House & Storey, 1: p. 481.
[12] Ley's note in Forster's *Life,* p. 328.
[13] George Gissing, *Charles Dickens* [1898] (New York, 1924), pp. 74-75.
[14] George Gissing, *Critical Studies in the Work of Charles Dickens* (New York, 1924), p. 101.

Turning to Shakespeare, we recall the lines in what we think of as his farewell epilogue:

> Gentle breath of yours my sails
> Must fill, or else my project fails,
> Which was to please. . . .

That his project was always to please, and the many as distinct from the few, is apparent when his plays are compared with other plays in the popular repertories. Whether he is following the lead of lesser playwrights or they are following his, the inference must remain, that he is giving the general public the kind of thing it wants. That such is not only true, but indeed too true, was the opinion of some of his contemporaries and of certain critics since. If Dickens was too willing to leave some things out, Shakespeare was too willing to put some things in. He knew well that the rule of decorum legislated against the intrusion of low comic characters in serious plays—

> A goodly hotch potch when vile russetings
> Are matched with monarchs and with mighty kings[15]—

but he put them in just the same: farcical rebels in a history play, Launce and his piddling dog in a romantic comedy, bibulous gravediggers in a tragedy, and the like. Robert Bridges, in his essay on the influence of Shakespeare's audience, refuses to forgive those "wretched beings" who prevented "the greatest poet and dramatist of the world from being the best artist."[16] His description of the public as "wretched beings" reveals that this high-minded laureate subscribes to the ideal described but not endorsed by Gissing. In the realm of art, the people corrupt.

If we view doctrines of elitism with more reserve, we may see something enviable in the position of Shake-

---
[15] Joseph Hall, *Virgidemiarum*, 1597, Satire 3.
[16] "On the Influence of the Audience," *The Works of William Shakespeare*, ed. A. H. Bullen (10 v., Stratford-upon-Avon, 1904-1907): **10**, p. 334.

speare and Dickens. They could measure success with a yardstick which did not shrink or stretch. If the public kept coming, there was only one thing more they needed to know. I shall turn to it in a moment. They were not inhibited by spectral analysts peering over their shoulders, by anxiety about prestige in superior circles, by fear of excommunication by this critical sect or that because of their popular ministry. Those pressures which distract an artist's attention from what he is doing to how he is doing it, and kill his heart by making him stand up prematurely beside the towering dead, were not intrusive in Shakespeare's day. There were no lectures or doctoral dissertations on contemporary writers, no literary journals, not even newspaper reviews. The invasion was well under way in Dickens's time but he held it stoutly at bay. Forster quotes his resolution "kept for twenty years" not to read critical complaints.[17] Singleness of purpose is a wonderful boon. Pity the serious writers of today, when popular success is associated with artistic failure but when popular failure is too easily achieved to be a reliable index of artistic success. Artists have nothing to lean on if they must hold in equal distrust the approval and disapproval of the public. This may be one of the reasons we have had so many maimed geniuses tracking out the footsteps of other maimed geniuses in various lands of exile.

Perhaps that same capacity for affection which made Shakespeare and Dickens put up with members of their families impelled them to put up with members of their race—willing, so to speak, to remain at home instead of restlessly seeking some more congenial Somewhere-else. However, we cannot let the matter rest here. When I said that they both had two sisters and three brothers, I was not saying that I had pierced

---

[17] *Life*, ed. Ley, p. 627.

to the heart of their mystery, and one need only have two sisters and three brothers to become a great writer. And I am not saying now that willingness and ability to please the many is a badge of artistic genius. Writers have had this willingness and ability, yet produced work wholly deplorable. What meaning the parallels I am tracing may have resides in the whole pattern, not in separate details. I turn now to what I consider the most significant detail in the pattern. Shakespeare and Dickens shared the amazing trait—amazing that is among popular writers—that they were not seduced by their success. They had to know, not only that their writing continued to please the public, but also that it continued to please themselves as the best they could do. In the case of Dickens this is a matter of copious record. In that of Shakespeare it is a matter of inference, and I shall treat it first.

A study of Shakespeare's texts shows that he sometimes improvised and was careless about inessential details. Contemporary comment shows that he had a reputation for facility. But neither the textual nor historical evidence supports the notion that he was the one genius who needed no capacity for taking pains, but found it *easy* to give his writing an appearance of *ease*. When the Prince (3, 2) speaks of groundlings as "capable of nothing but inexplicable dumb shows and noise," Shakespeare must have been expressing Hamlet's opinion rather than his own; otherwise his plays would have a piebald quality which is exactly what they have not. Their parts have a wide range of appeal, but there is no corresponding range in the quality of these parts, as if some were designed for the capacity of groundlings, others for that of two-penny patrons, and so on. Everything, including farcical rebels and drunken gravediggers, was designed to please everyone, including himself.

Thirty-six plays appear in the Folio. No other body of secular literature has been submitted to such intense scrutiny in regard to the question of authorship. The sum total of the findings, after long and laborious search, is that a few of the early plays may, and one late play does, contain writing by another hand. The homogeneity of this body of work is almost miraculous. Normally, during Shakespeare's career, scripts for the public theaters were turned out on assembly lines, with from two to six writers working on each play. Shakespeare and his company could have made as much money, perhaps more, if he had used his talents as play-doctor or directing member of the various teams working for the company. Jonson, though a committed poet, joined such teams occasionally, but he excluded from his printed works any play not written exclusively by himself. Shakespeare probably did serve sometimes as play-doctor, or as contributor of a scene or two to collaborative work, as suggested by the apparent appearance of his hand in the manuscript of *Sir Thomas More,* but the salient fact is that, unlike others, he rarely diluted himself in collaboration, but for almost twenty years wrote an average of two plays a year *alone*. As we examine these plays in relation to each other, we observe that he does not imitate his successes, but competes with them, never coasting, always striking out in new directions.

The smell of the lamp was absent from his work, and so he was classified as a Poet of Nature. Francis Beaumont said,

> And from all learning keep these lines as clear
> As Shakespeare's best are which our heirs shall hear,[18]

and his fellow actors, Hemming and Condell, "His

---

[18]"To Mr. B.J.," in E. K. Chambers, *William Shakespeare* (2 v., Oxford, 1930) **2**: p. 224.

mind and his hand went together, and what he thought he uttered, with that easiness that we have scarce received from him a blot in his papers."[19] From this it is only a step to Milton's picture of him in *L'Allegro* as "Fancy's child" warbling "his native woodnotes wild." Jonson attacked this myth at the very moment of its inception. When he snapped at Hemming and Condell, "Would he had blotted a thousand," he was not saying that Shakespeare had spent too little creative energy, but rather that he had spent too much: "Sufflaminandus erat."[20] He had in fact contradicted the notion that Shakespeare wrote with effortless facility in the very volume in which it was offered as a compliment:

> Who casts a living line must sweat,
>   Such as thine are, and strike the second heat
> Upon the Muse's anvil; turn the same
>   And himself with it, that he thinks to frame.[21]

Jonson is here telling us what must be true, that Shakespeare turned himself on the anvil. The idea that his plays were written at a cost incommensurate with their quality has never made much sense.

As to Dickens, the whole gravamen of Forster's account of his writing career, and everything we learn from his private correspondence attest to his willingness to burn himself up to sustain the quality of his writing. He did not always succeed. Exhaustion sometimes led to inferior work, but at such times he had to delude himself: he could not bring himself to publish anything he recognized as inferior. Athough always supplying letterpress in stated amounts at stated intervals, he never became a hack. One of the curiosities of

---

[19]"To the Great Variety of Readers," Shakespeare Folio (1623).
[20]"De Shakespeare nostrati," *Timber: or Discoveries* (1641). Forster (*Life*, ed. Ley, p. 477) applies Jonson's remarks to Dickens.
[21]"To the memory of my beloved. . . ," Shakespeare Folio (1623).

literary history is the way in which his attitude differs from that of the two comparably voluminous novelists of the century, Scott and Trollope. Although both were true-blue gentry, and admirably committed as citizens to the ideal of *noblesse oblige,* both treated their creative gift as they might have treated any other financial asset. Scott did not revise, but just wrote and wrote as he added to the acreage of Abbotsford, while Trollope said often and openly that his aim was to give value for value received, like any reliable tailor, cobbler, or coffin-maker.[22] In contrast, although he fought for every shilling due him, the writing of novels was for Dickens a mission and act of faith.

In an essay called "Two Views of a Cheap Theatre" he indirectly states his creed, that ordinary people should be given the best and that they have the capacity to rise to it. When the new Britannia Theatre opened, he went to watch the audience. The bulk of it, while not actually crude, was far from refined, and he draws it in unsparing detail. He is amused at its lively response to the pantomime and melodrama, but there is not a trace of contempt in his tone. The next night, a Sunday, he returned. An attempt was being made to improve the morals of London by bringing the gospel message to the populace. The Britannia is again thronged because admission is free, but the response is now apathetic. Dickens puts the blame squarely on the preacher, whose way of talking down he clearly hates although he treats it with his usual comic relish. Then he says something which throws light, innocently I believe, upon his own achievement: "In this congregation there is undubitably one pulse, but I doubt if any power short of genius could touch it as one, and make it answer as one." But he is sure that it could be done.

---

[22]Anthony Trollope, *An Autobiography,* ed. M. Sadleir & F. Page (Oxford, 1950), p. 357 *et passim.*

The trouble is not with those who fail to pick up the pearls of the gospel narrative but with those who are casting them:

> Let the preacher who will thoroughly forget himself . . . stand up before four thousand men and women at the Britannia Theatre any Sunday night, recounting that narrative to them as fellow creatures, and he will see a sight![23]

It is always moving to hear the voice of someone who does not talk about the worth of the Common Man, but who seems truly to believe in the worth of the men and women in actual view.

The word *entertainer* is in such ill repute among critics that they would no sooner apply it to a great writer than they would apply the word *decorator* to a great painter. But some great painters have been decorators, rising to great occasions as they adorned certain walls and ceilings. We must accept the possibility that an occasional fine writer might consider each chance to entertain thousands of his fellow creatures as a great occasion. Ben Jonson was not such a man—he trusted only the "judicious"—but he considered his vocation sacred. In his eyes a hack, a writer who gave

---

[23] The essay, which originally appeared in *All the Year Round,* is collected in The *Uncommercial Traveller.* When I was writing *Shakespeare's Audience* (1941) and speculating on the social make-up of the one-penny patrons and how they were probably self-policed, I had not read this piece or I would have quoted the following passage:

"Besides prowlers and idlers, we were mechanics, dock laborers, coster-mongers, petty tradesmen, small clerks, milliners, stay-makers, shoe-binders, slop-workers, poor workers in a hundred highways and by-ways. Many of us—on the whole the majority—were not at all clean, and not at all choice in our lives or conversation. But we had all come together in a place where our convenience was well consulted, and where we were well looked after, to enjoy an evening's entertainment in common. We were not going to lose any part of what we had paid for through anybody's caprice, and as a community we had a character to lose. So, we were closely attentive, and kept excellent order: and let the man or boy who did otherwise instantly get out from this place, or we would put him out with the greatest expedition."

Another essay, animated by the same spirit, appears in the same volume, "The Boiled Beef of New England," but best of all is the defense of the literary and musical aspirations of the Lowell factory girls in *American Notes* (chap. 4).

less than his best, was a "rogue" as distinct from an honest poet. He was a carping, envious, suspicious fellow, with a gimlet eye for fraud, but his final verdict on Shakespeare was, "He was indeed honest."[24] Thomas Carlyle was another curmudgeon, skeptical, waspish, disdainful of novelists as a class, and hence a little ashamed of his fondness for Dickens, but his final verdict on this particular novelist was, ". . . every inch of him an Honest Man!"[25] The integrity of artists cannot be established on the basis of testimonials, but we must be impressed when they come from men like Jonson and Carlyle, who found it hard to believe that an entertainer of the market place, a charmer of the throng, could nevertheless be *honest.*

4

My object is to define a kind of power. What I have tried to do thus far would be wasted effort, even if it proved that Shakespeare and Dickens were virtually the same person, if designed to demonstrate that they possessed power. This needs no demonstration. Power is measurable, and we need only read the dials to see these two as the most powerful of imaginative writers in English. Each was the recognized champion in his own times. When we seek out the best sellers of various periods, we always come up with disconcerting finds. The most popular single Elizabethan play was not one of Shakespeare's, not *Hamlet,* but Kyd's *Spanish Tragedy.* The most popular single novel in Victorian England was not one of Dickens's, not *Pickwick Papers,* but Stowe's *Uncle Tom's Cabin.* Nevertheless, Shakespeare and Dickens were the overall best sellers, with the largest following in all sectors of the general public

---

[24]"De Shakespeare nostrati."
[25]Letter to Forster, June 11, 1970, quoted by Edgar Johnson, *Charles Dickens* (2 v., New York, 1952), p. 1155.

and the highest reputation in the literary community. The idea that literary power is not recognized during an author's lifetime is a consoling notion among those who have failed with the general public, or with the critics, or both. The general public or the critics may be wrong, and often are, but when the two agree they are never wrong. Such agreement is rare. There has been no writer in this century who has been crowned as a champion by both.

The power of these two has been proven also by their ability to break through geographic and linguistic barriers. Often the first time we hear of some strange foreign tongue is when we read that Shakespeare's plays have been translated into it. Dickens's vogue abroad was instantaneous. His novels have become classics in many lands, including those in the Soviet bloc; and we are constantly hearing of novelists as different from him and from each other as Tolstoy, Dostoevsky, Proust, Joyce, and Kafka who were under obligation to him. Finally they have shown power to endure. No one will dispute the fact that of all plays of the past, Shakespeare's are now the most often performed, and of all novels of the past, Dickens's now the most often read.

The kind of power these two shared may indeed be related to the kind of men they were, their circumstances, and their aims; but definition must rely finally upon critical analysis. Horace long ago proposed the *dulce et utile* test. The poets, the makers, win the hearts of men if they offer the sweet and the useful, both profit and delight. I have one entire hour in which to offer an analysis of Shakespeare's and Dickens's artistry, to indicate the means by which it delights. Then comes the question of usefulness, or moral value. Poets trade in feeling, not fact, and whether feeling has any moral value at all is a moot point. Still, my topic is not what kind of feeling is useful, but what kind has *seemed* useful to those over whom these particular writers have exercised their power—so many people, in so many places, through so many years.

II. Art To Enchant

1

THOSE who have searched for Shakespeare and Dickens among their characters have most often discovered the playright in Prospero the Enchanter, and the novelist in the Spirit of Christmas Present sprinkling incense from his magic horn. The tendency to see their artistry as magic goes back a long time. In his elegiac tribute, Jonson said that Shakespeare came forth—

>   . . . to warm
> Our ears, or like a Mercury to charm.

Josiah Quincy, Jr., when he presented Dickens at the first American banquet in his honor, quoted Falstaff's charge that Prince Hal had given him love charms: "If the rascal have not given me medicines to make me love him, I'll be hanged. It could not be else: I have drunk medicines."[1] Even the critics who now propose a Shakespeare come forth to chill continue to see him as Prospero, although in robes dyed modern black. Edmund Wilson's Dickens dispenses potions less benign than love charms, but he remains a mighty magician.

I shall be speaking presently of "word magic," and of the kind of sorcery which endows puppets with the appearance of life, but I must begin with a word about the kind of wonder-world to which both of these writers conduct us. Of the books he read when he was young, the one which seems to have left the firmest imprint on Shakespeare's mind was Ovid's *Metamorphoses*, a book of wonder. If asked to characterize in a

---

[1] W. G. Wilkins, *Charles Dickens in America* (London, 1911), p. 24.

single phrase the folio of his works, I would call it a book of wonder. In it are many marvels: a shrew metamorphosed into a meek and loving wife, an earth-blighting quarrel between the tiny king and queen of fairyland, a suitor who wins a golden bride by choosing a leaden casket, a remnant army which slays ten thousand Frenchmen at the cost of only twenty-five English lives, a ghost in armor who haunts the battlements and bedrooms of Elsinore, a wood which marches on Dunsinane, a penitent and his child to whom the wife and mother they mourn is restored in the form of a living statue, and so on. The fabulousness of these stories is not merely a reflection of the archaic nature of fiction at the time. Other kinds of material were available, as the satirical realists pointed out. The stories Shakespeare retold were the kind he preferred. Those he invented himself are even more wonderful in cast than those he borrowed from others.

Of the books which Dickens read when young, the one which seems to have impressed him most was also a book of wonder, *The Arabian Nights Entertainments,* and the folio of his works, if one can imagine a volume four times the bulk of Shakespeare's, might be similarly described. He was forced by the tradition of the novel to invent his own stories and to give them realistic settings; hence we depart only in excursions from sooty London and a few towns in provincial England. There are no Bohemian seacoasts, no enchanted woods or islands, no haunted castles except prisons, indeed no ghosts for haunting except in the dreams of a Scrooge or Trotty Veck. Nevertheless, Dickens offers as many marvels as Shakespeare: a portly figure of fun metamorphosed into an "angel in gaiters," the Odyssean journeys of children through bizarre realms of peril, a cleansing descent into the Hades of the American frontier, a drunkard who melts away in spontaneous combustion, a house which collapses of moral rot, a man who substitutes himself for his double condemned to the guillotine, another who mingles watchfully among those who think he has died, and so on again.

Dickens's strange events are not Shakespeare's, but their generic kinship is indisputable. In both authors the same motifs appear repeatedly: the Haroun al-Raschid motif of the secret adjudicator, the fairy-godmother motif of the weird benefactor, the equally ancient motifs of the lost-child-recovered, the maligned innocent, beauty and the beast, the self-destroying destroyer, and the like. Providence is an unseen character who moves on the stages of both, without offense, because most of us, in spite of our rational orthodoxy, still believe in Good Luck, meaning luck for the good. Coincidence, concealed identity, deceptive role-playing, sudden conversion, occur as commonly in the one author as in the other. The change of heart of old Scrooge is no more implausible than that of Duke Angelo; and the success of Vincentio in the role of friar no more so than the success of John Harmon in the role of Boffin's clerk. The waif Perdita is abandoned on the one Mediterranean shore which her mother would have chosen, and the waif Oliver is thrust by burglars into the one house in England which *his* mother would have chosen. The drowned body of Steerforth lies on those Yarmouth sands where he had seduced Emily, and some silent Ariel guides Canon Crisparkle to the very spot where Edwin Drood's stickpin may be seen glittering in the Cloisterham weir. In Dickens as in Shakespeare dire events are marked by Nature's auguries. There are no "late eclipses of the sun and moon," no showers of meteors, no cannibalistic horses, but there are fogs enveloping the Court of Chancery, imprisoning gray skies and mists over the marshlands where convicts lurk, black tides in the Thames yielding up the bodies of suicides and murdered men. In both authors tempests sound a protest against moral disorder, and signal the approach of Nemesis.

The nature of their material does not in itself explain their appeal. Folk themes and thrilling action can be less a sign of primitive strength than of creative debility. Marvels in plenty were vended in Elizabethan puppet-plays and broadsides, and by Victorian impresarios who wrapped up farce, melodrama, and pantomime in single cheap packages. It may be argued that portentous subject matter, especially when fancifully presented, may serve as a substitute for artistry. One is forced to take interest in the rescue of an innocent boy like Oliver from a den of thieves, or an innocent girl like Marina from pirates and a brothel; or in the perpetration and punishment of murder by a Macbeth or Bill Sikes. The greater feat is Jane Austen's, or even Anthony Trollope's, who can make us read through three volumes to learn whether the vicar's worthy daughter will at last win a proposal from Lord Wishbone. But we are not here considering categories of writers who succeed, but two particular writers who succeeded greatly. Those who choose universal themes put themselves in universal competition, and can only excel by making the old seem new. What distinguishes the wonder-worlds of Shakespeare and Dickens is that there breathes about them the freshness of the first creation. Moral consistency gives them inner cohesion, and an abundance of convincing detail gives them solidity. We are offered illusions we can delight in as shows, with vivid coloring, strong stage lighting, and an accentuation of the solemn and the absurd, but we are also offered revelation—shows with their own kind of veracity.

2

How is it done? It is done with a mosaic of mirrors, cunningly chosen and articulated words. The literary illusionist has nothing else to work with. If Shakespeare upon retirement buried "deeper than did ever plummet sound" a book equivalent to Prospero's how-to manual for magicians, it would have been a giant lexicon. The most unarguable thing we can say about his use of words is that he used a great variety of them. His working vocabulary was larger than those of all other playwrights in his time, including the university-trained. The makers of concordances have not yet been busy enough with nineteenth-century writers to let us make firm assertions, but my guess is that when the computers have finished their researches, we shall find that Dickens's working vocabulary was larger than those of all other novelists in his time, and considerably larger than Shakespeare's. He had assimilated while still young nearly all the words which remained current in Shakespeare, and was able to draw upon the vastly increased English stock. Practically everything visible in Victorian England is named somewhere or other in Dickens, including a host of things non-existent in Elizabethan times. The mere number of words used is not in itself an index of excellence—a neo-classical writer like Racine, who favors categorical diction, achieves his effects with relatively few—but in the case of the writers we are considering quantity is related to quality. Their vocabularies had to be large because of their habit of indicating the general by means of the specific, constructing ideas with concrete details.

When the witches in *Macbeth* boil their ghastly stew, they chant the recipe, which includes fillet of swamp snake. The word "fillet" is used here (4, 1) and here only in Shakespeare; it was in his head awaiting just this occasion. When Macbeth argues (3, 1) that men act according to kind, like dogs, he specifies eight breeds of dogs. Three of these, shoughs, water-rugs, and demi-wolves, are mentioned nowhere else in his works. We are told (2, 1) that the bank where Titania lies is covered with wild thyme, oxlips, violets, woodbine, musk-roses, and eglantine. The grieving Ophelia speaks (4, 5) of rosemary, pansies, fennel, columbine, rue, violets, and daisies. Lear in his madness (4, 4) wears a crown of fumiter, furrow weeds, hardocks, hemlock, nettles, darnel and cuckoo flowers. The word "violets" is mentioned twice in these lists; there are no other repetitions. When Perdita speaks (4, 4) of her gardening, violets are again mentioned, as well as oxlips, rosemary, and rue, but there are twelve additional items: carnations, gillivors, lavendar, mints, savory, marjoram, marigolds, daffodils, primroses, the crown imperial, the flower-de-luce, and lilies. These inventories, properly fitted to proper occasions, must be recognized as the natural precipitant of a style concrete to the point of saturation. By being specific, Shakespeare is able to make his world seem more real, or at least more substantial, than the world of the realists. Titania is not a realistic character, but the wild thyme, oxlips, violets, woodbine, musk-roses, and eglantine on which she lies confer their reality upon her. So also do the woodland pests from which her tiny guards defend her—not categorized as "pests" but specified (2, 2) as newts, spiders, spinners, beetles, worms, blind-worms, and snails.

Dickens is specific in precisely the same way, and even more prone to itemizing. To enter a shop with him, grocer's, taxidermist's, rag-and-bone dealer's, is to get an inventory of the stock in trade. To meet one of his characters is to get an inventory of that character's apparel, with notes on its state of repair. When he tells of seven-year-old lovers who elope, he naturally lists their luggage: hers consisting of a parasol, a smelling-bottle, some cold buttered toast, eight peppermint drops, and a doll's hairbrush; his consisting of about six yards of string, a knife, several sheets of writing paper folded very small, an orange, and a china mug with his name on it.[2] Why items so random should seem so authentic is part of this artist's mystery; he could even see into children's pockets. To perceive how there can be similarity of method applied to totally dissimilar material, we need only turn from Shakespeare's flowers to Dickens' lists of food. His devilish gnome Quilp rivals Shakespeare's witches in the oddity of his diet; he breakfasts (1, 5) upon boiling tea, huge prawns with their heads and tails on, hard-boiled eggs shells and all, and watercress spiced with tobacco. In *Little Dorrit* Monsieur Rigaud, Mrs. Clennam, and Mr. Casby are each served a meal shortly after we first meet them.[3] The wily operator Rigaud eats well even in his Marseilles prison-cell; sausage wrapped in vine leaf, Lyons veal in savory jelly, three small rolls of white bread, and vintage wine. The imaginary invalid Mrs. Clennam has her usual mid-morning "refection": oysters circularly arranged on a white dish and covered with a white cloth, a slice of buttered French roll, and a small glass of chilled wine and water. The unctuous slumlord Casby has a regular Casby dinner: soup, fried soles, a butter-boat of shrimp sauce, potatoes, mutton, a steak, and apple pie, preceded by sherry, accompanied by porter, and followed by port, all of which he consumes "with the benignity of a good soul . . . feeding some one else." This concreteness is as appropriately variable as Shakespeare's and it functions in the

---

[2] "The Boots," *The Holly Tree* (2).
[3] Book 1, chaps. 1, 5, 13.

same paradoxical way, authenticating the implausible. The realistic novelists coeval with Dickens often tell us that their characters dine but rarely what they dine on. He always tells us, realizing that we might like to know, and also that abstract meals are untrue to life. Even his most fantastic characters, like Quilp, are real presences, never wraiths; certainly never so "flat" as to lack capacious organs of digestion.

Words such as "violets" or "oysters" trigger the formation of images in our minds. The double-triggering effected when these images are linked with each other, and with ideas, sentiments, emotions, in the interest of definition, enhancement, emphasis, is known by the general term *imagery*. When the Elizabethans spoke of "wit" and the Victorians of "invention," they usually meant what we usually mean when we speak of "creative *imagination*"—the gift of certain persons with well-stocked and agile minds to communicate to others their perception of relationships. The poet is "of imagination all compact" but, unlike the madman or lover, he remains the master of it. Shakespeare and Dickens were of imagination more "compact" than other English playwrights and novelists, the most able to vivify and vitalize their writing with imagery. Shakespeare's pictorial mode of communication, his puns and wordplay, have received much critical attention. Dickens's imagery, his wordplay, his puns, will offer an equally inexhaustible mine when critics get around to working it. I can give only a token treatment of this complex subject.

Both writers constantly let the animate and inanimate worlds interpenetrate, also the human and non-human.[4] In Shakespeare "sails grow big-bellied,"

---

[4]Caroline Spurgeon (*Shakespeare's Imagery*, Cambridge Univ. Press, 1952) provides statistical proof that Shakespeare's images are drawn primarily from natural objects. We need no statistical proof to know that Dickens's images are drawn

made pregnant by the "wanton wind"; the stars at dawn are "night's candles . . . burnt out"; and the silks from a wrecked argosy "enrobe the roaring waters."[5] In Dickens the stealthy night-wind tries "with unseen hand the windows and the doors"; gaslights turned on early because of fog "have a haggard and unwilling look"; and elm trees bending toward each other are "giants . . . whispering secrets."[6] A reverse exchange of properties occurs when Hal sees Falstaff round as a "huge bombard of sack" and conspicuous as St. Paul's Cathedral, and when Copperfield sees Heep leaving snail tracks on the books he fingers or casting on the Wickfield home the shadow of a giant bat.[7] As employed by these masters, the images have multiple im-

---

primarily from man-made objects and that, compared with him, Shakespeare might almost be called a pastoralist. The most influential study of Dickens's imagery is Dorothy Van Ghents's ("The Dickens World: A View from Todgers," *Sewanee Review*, 1950), in which material is presented to illustrate his habit of giving human beings the insensate quality of things, and things the deformities of human beings. Since the images assembled in the essay convey an impression of misanthropy and morbidity, we must ask why readers have seen in the novels the reverse of these qualities. The question was asked early, even with reference to the "view" from Todgers, in discussion of the "Hogarthian" nature of Dickens's art (see T. H. Lister, *Edinburgh Review* **68**, 1838; and R. H. Horne, *A New Spirit of the Age* **1**, 1844) and was answered in somewhat contradictory ways—by denying that Dickens's art *was* Hogarthian, and by denying that Hogarth's was morbid or misanthropic. Other answers suggest themselves. Actually a fair number of Dickens's images are drawn from nature, and things are not always given human deformities. For instance, the view of a Wiltshire village, which also occurs in *Martin Chuzzlewit* (1, 2), is quite different from the view from Todgers: from its windows at evening ". . . such gleams of light shone back upon the gleaming sky, that it seemed as if the quiet buildings were the hoarding places of twenty summers, and all their mildness and warmth were stored within." The city-country antithesis, traditional in literature, prevails in the novels in spectacular form because the nineteenth-century Coketowns and London slums were truly ghastly places. We must still ask why the kind of images Van Ghent assembles do not in their context spread gloom. Perhaps we should think less of the young Dickens walking the London streets in dread and more of the still younger Dickens reading the *Arabian Nights* in wonder. He creates a demonic world, but it has stimulated rather than depressed readers because of a tacit bargain he has made with them that he will bring his wayfarers through it safely. Moreover it is dotted with havens, and peopled by more than ogres. Todgers itself is a remarkably cheerful place in spite of the view.

[5]*Midsummer Night's Dream* (1, 1), *Romeo and Juliet* (3, 5), *Merchant of Venice* (1, 1).
[6]*The Chimes* (chap. 1), *Bleak House* (1, 1), *David Copperfield* (1, 1).
[7]*I Henry IV* (2, 4), *David Copperfield* (1, 16; 2, 20).

plications. Scrooge sees his door-knocker transform itself into the face of his dead partner Marley, with "a dismal light about it, like a bad lobster in a dark cellar." We may think the writer is only indulging in comic incongruitty until we realize that he is invoking the idea of a face after burial, with the stench and phosphorescent glow of decay. Let us "laugh at that"—in Hamlet's words as he addresses the skull of Yorick. Throughout Scrooge's later interview with the ghost there is a play of ideas and images showing Dickens's Shakespearean tendency to blend the homely and grotesque, the facetious and macabre; to greet horror with a pun. "Ask for me to-morrow," says the dying Mercutio, "and you shall find me a grave man." The quaking Scrooge tells the ghost it is only a dream bred of indigestion: "There's more of gravy than of grave about you. . . ." The ghost's loud groans alternating with Scrooge's bad jokes are an eerie counterpart of those which greet puns at jolly parties.

The imagery is not always responsibly "functional." Like Shakespeare in the person of Berowne, Mercutio, and others, Dickens often plays with words purely in a spirit of play, exuberantly and with delight in his own ingenuity. The green paper covers of his serial numbers license him to speak of the green "leaves" he puts out monthly, and the public's appreciation as the "genial sun and showers that have fallen on these leaves."[8] The cordials stored in a house in the close, "having been for ages hummed through by the cathedral bell and organ," are now "sublimated honey" so that dippers emerge from them with faces mellowed as by a "saccharine transfiguration"; a passionate youth tossing his long dusty hair over eyes and ears has a wild appearance "similar to a blasted heath"; and the grainy portraits produced by the photographers of the day

---

[8]*David Copperfield,* author's preface.

make the subject look "like a new-ploughed field."⁹ As in Shakespeare the line between jest and earnest is hard to draw. The nighttime gloom of a railway junction is truly conveyed by mention of "Mysterious goods trains, covered with palls and gliding on like vast weird funerals," but what shall we say of the coal cars appended to trains in the switching yard, stopping, backing, advancing like detectives shadowing their prey?¹⁰ "Sufflaminandus erat." Still, one of the joys of rereading Dickens as well as Shakespeare lies in relishing the sheer fertility of his mind.

Normally the writing of both is firmly disciplined, pleasing us with order as well as energy, with rhetorical artifice as well as graphic richness. Every device in the classical and Renaissance manuals, every variety of parallelism, antithesis, climactic arrangement, was used by Shakespeare to provide clarity, emphasis, and pleasing symmetry. Patterned modes of expression were less widely espoused in the nineteenth century, but Dickens proves on scrutiny to have been as artful a rhetorician as Shakespeare. Again, only token illustration can be offered here. Perhaps the device least difficult to treat orally is that of verbal repetition with ironic intent. In dispersed form it gives us "honest" Iago, and "humble" Uriah Heep. Clustered, it gives us the "honorable" assassins of Caesar, and the "respectable" Mr. Littimer. Littimer is Steerforth's valet, Dickens's version of the type represented in Shakespeare by Goneril's Oswald—a demure sycophant pandering to the vices of his employer. Littimer's name and appearance are quite neutral, but when he is described as "respectable" nine times in the paragraph in which he is introduced,¹¹ we are fully prepared to find him despicable.

---

[9]*Edwin Drood* (chap. 1), *Somebody's Luggage* (chap. 4), *Mrs. Lirriper's Lodgings* (chap. 1).
[10]*Mugby Junction* (chap. 1).
[11]*David Copperfield* (2, 2).

The following passage sustaining the repetition of two words, but climactically abandoning the repetition of a third, is filled with ruses common in Shakespeare. Incidentally it is built on a reminiscence of Othello's dismissive, "yet that's not much," after he wonders (3, 3) if he could have lost Desdemona's love because he has declined somewhat into "the vale of years." Arthur Clennam in middle age meets his youthful flame, Flora Finching, and is saddened to find her declined into the vale of years:

> Flora, always tall, had grown to be very broad too, and short of breath; but that was not much. Flora, whom he had left a lily, had become a peony; but that was not much. Flora, who had seemed enchanting in all she said and thought, was diffusee and silly. That was much. Flora, who had been spoiled and artless long ago, was determined to be spoiled and artless now. That was a fatal blow.[12]

Shakespeare was a lord of language, molding it to his will. He wrote in many styles—Shylock's, Falstaff's, Bottom's, Hamlet's—yet the style was always his own. That Dickens was also a lord of language, a great stylist, has not always been recognized. In a way this is a token of his success: even his critical readers have sometimes been so subject to his legerdemain that they have failed to notice that it is, in last analysis, verbal. George Henry Lewes was able to say that he lacked "charm of composition" in the very sentence in which he said we enjoy his writing "like children at play, laughing and crying at the images which pass before us. . . ."[13] How he accounted for the potency of these images Lewes does not say. Dickens, too, wrote in many styles—Sam Weller's, Micawber's, Sarah Gamp's, Mrs. Lirriper's—all different but all his own. He could write in the stately style of an Augustan essayist; as in

---

[12]*Little Dorrit* (1, 13).
[13]"Dickens in Relation to Criticism," *The Dickens Critics*, ed. G. H. Ford & L. Lane Jr. (Ithaca, 1961), p. 73.

the following passage from *The Uncommercial Traveller* (chap. 27) on incurable discontent:

> As I have known legatees deeply injured by a bequest of five hundred pounds because it was not five thousand, and as I was once acquainted with a pensioner on the Public, to the extent of two hundred a year, who perpetually anathematized his Country because he was not in the receipt of four, having no claim whatever to six-pence; so perhaps it usually happens, within certain limits, that to get a little help is to get a notion of being defrauded of more. "How do they pass their lives in this beautiful and peaceful place?" was the subject of my speculation with a visitor who once accompanied me to a charming rustic retreat for old men and women;; a quaint ancient foundation in a pleasant English county, behind a picturesque church, and among rich old convent gardens. There were but some dozen or so of houses, and we agreed that we would talk with the inhabitants, as they sat in their groined rooms between the light of their fires and the light shining in at their latticed windows, and would find out. They passed their lives in considering themselves mulcted of certain ounces of tea by a deaf old steward who lived among them in the quadrangle. There was no reason to suppose that any such ounces of tea had ever been in existence, or that the old steward so much as knew what was the matter;—he passed *his* life in considering himself periodically defrauded of a birch-broom by the beadle.

In this passage we have been given a place, its people, its atmosphere, together with a universal truth and a joke, so that, in spite of its leisurely rhythms, it meets the test of superior writing; offering "riches in a little room." True, it has about it an air of performance, but so do some of the soliloquies of Shakespeare.

At the opposite extreme are passages so offhand and racy as to defy literary decorum—as in the description in *Little Dorrit* (1, 6) of a doctor of the Marshalsea, who is called on to serve at a childbirth in a family of fellow debtors:

> The turnkey, opening the door, disclosed, in a wretched, ill-smelling little room, two hoarse, puffy, red-faced personages, seated at a rickety table, playing at all-fours, smoking pipes, and drinking brandy.

"Doctor," said the turnkey, "here's a gentleman's wife in want of you without a minute's loss of time."

The doctor's friend was in the positive degree of hoarseness, puffiness, redfacedness, all-fours, tobacco, dirt, and brandy; the doctor in the comparative—hoarser, puffier, more red-faced, more all-foury, tobaccoer, dirtier, and brandier. The doctor was amazingly shabby, in a torn and darned rough-weather sea-jacket, out at elbows, and eminently short of buttons (he had been in his time the experienced surgeon carried by a passenger ship), the dirtiest white trousers conceivable by mortal man, carpet slippers, and no visible linen. "Childbed?" said the doctor, "I'm the boy!" With that the doctor took a comb from the chimney-piece, and stuck his hair upright—which appeared to be his way of washing himself—produced a professional chest or case, of most abject appearance, from the cupboard where his cup and saucer and coals were, settled his chin in the frowzy wrapper round his neck, and became a ghastly medical practitioner.

"All-foury"? "Tobaccoer"? "Brandier"? We can understand Trollope's complaint that Dickens's prose was "jerky, ungrammatical, and created by himself in defiance of rules."[14] Still, this is precisely what a similarly sensible Elizabethan author would have said of Shakespeare's verse. The lords of language do not defy rules. They only seem to do so, as they follow more exacting rules of their own decree.[15]

---

[14] *An autobiography*, ed. M. Sadleir & F. Page (Oxford, 1950), p. 249.

[15] Dickens's later style, like Shakespeare's, is often marked by a remarkable density of detail. In the following brief passage (1, 6) from *Hard Times*, 1854 (as unconventional as that quoted above from *Little Dorrit*, 1855-1857), Dickens draws two performers and their act, at an increasing rate of speed, like that with which they circled the ring at Sleary's horse-carnival:

". . . a young man appeared at the door, and, introducing himself with the words 'By your leaves, gentlemen!' walked in, with his hands in his pockets. His face, close-shaven, thin, and sallow, was shaded by a great quantity of dark hair, brushed into a roll all round his head, and parted up the centre. His legs were very robust, but shorter than legs of good proportion should have been. His chest and back were as much too broad as his legs were too short. He was dressed in a Newmarket coat and tight-fitting trousers; wore a shawl round his neck; smelt of lamp-oil, straw, orange-peel, horse's provender, and sawdust; and looked a most remarkable sort of Centaur, compounded of the stable and the playhouse. Where the one began and the other ended, nobody could have told with any precision. This gentleman was mentioned in the bills of the day as Mr. E. W. B. Childers, so justly celebrated for his daring vaulting act as the Wild Huntsman of the North American Prairies; in which popular performance a diminutive boy with an old

3

Forged in the imagination of these writers, episodes and characters often greet us with the vivid immediacy of hallucination, and yet function like extended metaphors, universalizing the particular. At least once in each of the greater Shakespearean plays, an event seems suspended in time, like the perpetual re-enactment of some central human experience. The scene where Romeo and Juliet first plight their faith both illustrates and defines young love. The scene where Macbeth steals, dagger in hand, to the chamber of Duncan both depicts a murder and Murder itself. So with key sequences in Dickens. The first great chapter in *Bleak House* invests a single sitting in the Court of Chancery with the quality of a recurring nightmare of frustration. The third stave of *A Christmas Carol,* taking us past snow-mantled London shops to watch the Cratchit family at dinner, is both a detailed genre picture and a master plan—of Saturnalia Christian-style.

Still more uncanny is the impact of some of the characters. What is meant by a "Shylock" or a "Scrooge" is known to many who never read a book. Of such escapees from literature to popular myth more have been created by Shakespeare and Dickens than by all their contemporaries combined. It is absurd to attribute their power to mere exaggeration and obviousness. Charges of lack of subtlety, or psychological truth, come from those who prefer a more literal kind of portraiture, but a greater show of accuracy

---

face, who now accompanied him, assisted as his infant son: being carried upside down over his father's shoulder, by one foot, and held by the crown of his head, heels upward, in the palm of his father's hand, according to the violent paternal manner in which wild huntsmen may be observed to fondle their offspring. Made up with curls, wreaths, white bismuth, and carmine, this hopeful young person soared into so pleasing a Cupid as to constitute the chief delight of the maternal part of the spectators; but in private, where his characteristics were a precocious cutaway coat and extremely gruff voice, he became of the Turf turfy."

does not always mean a greater impression of genuineness. There is a flaw in the "realistic" method. We do not come to know actual people by reading transcripts of the thoughts passing through their minds, or analytical passages on their psyches. Shakespeare as a dramatist was compelled to deal with externals, the visible and the audible. His characters are revealed to us in what they do, what they say, the way they say things, and their impact on each other. There are no editorial dissections. We must observe and piece together surface clues to subsurface characteristics. We must make deductions just as we must in actual life. The characters are, in a measure, the product of our curiosity and imagination, obvious in some ways, baffling in others, never pigeon-holed and inert.

Dickens used the dramatic method in writing his novels, and did so consciously.[16] He describes a character's physical features and mannerisms, costumes him, and provides appropriate scenery. From this point on the character is what he does, what he says, the way he says things, and the way he fits into his milieu. Whatever we know about how Mrs. Nickleby and Flora Finching think, we learn by hearing them talk. We have been told that Flora is "diffuse," but as we float on her stream of consciousness, we sometimes think we are navigating subterranean reaches, sometimes doubt if such reaches exist. The freely associated items in her and Mrs. Nickleby's discourse remind us of the reported ruminations of Leopold and Molly Bloom but function in a different way, not as inside information but only as supplementary surface data.

---

[16]The novelist "writes in effect for the stage." See "The Royal General Theatrical Fund," May 29, 1858 (*Speeches,* ed. Fielding, p. 262.) R. H. Horne (see above, note 4) was an early commentator upon his dramatic method of character creation as well as upon his anthropomorphic imagery. Forster always stressed the self-revelatory nature of his characters, and Gissing noted that he failed whenever he attempted to present them analytically.

Even the characters who tell their own stories seem to be speaking publicly, not privately, and when a character's thoughts are presented in detail, we usually find that we are reading not secrets of the soul but a discussion of the character's ethical dilemma. Nevertheless, as in Shakespeare, the treatment of surfaces can have the reverse of a superficial effect.

The young heroes, an Orlando or a Nickleby, are in neither writer the characters who impress us most; they are adequate to the purpose. The young heroines pose a special problem, which I shall treat in my discussion of ethical content. Of other characters there is one category where comparison is impossible. Dickens created no epic or majestic figures acting out their parts in the center of national or world stages. The closest he comes (and it is not close) is such a fallen conqueror in the realm of finance as Mr. Merdle of *Little Dorrit*. He can give Merdle a touch of dignity, and more than a touch of mystery[17] as in some degree the victim of his victims, but he cannot bring himself to give such a man heroic or tragic stature. The reason is that he himself did not respond emotionally to the idea of conquerors, with awe for those who succeed or pity for those who fail. This seems a limitation since most of us are more primitive than he in our feeling about symbols of conquest. On the other hand he excels all

---

[17]The public, speculators and non-speculators, because of the fascination of money, have made a myth of Mr. Merdle, and Dickens invests him with some of the qualities of a myth; but there are other reasons for the lasting impression he leaves with us. We never see into his mind, and we are puzzled by certain traits, for instance his shyness of manner and his conversational reticence—the reverse of what we might expect in a Herculean confidence man. We are reminded of those "inconsistencies" which make Shakespearean characters memorable. An opportunity to observe Dickens's method is offered by the contrast Merdle presents with Mr. Melmotte in Trollope's *The Way We Live Now*. The two play identical roles: Trollope's character also commits suicide after his fraudulent empire collapses. However, Melmotte is presented with explicit realism, as a ruthless, aggressive, and resourceful operator. We follow his career with keen interest, but having learned everything about him there is to learn, we soon forget him. He is not a *haunting* figure.

other writers in dealing with the opposite side of the human spectrum, that is, in portraying children. Forster's statement that he saw people *invisible* to others, such as waiters, grooms, ticket porters, really applies also to children. Older writers, even Shakespeare, saw children as did the painters, either as undersized adults or as conventionally pathetic or cute. Dickens saw them as individuals, and quite without sentimentality. He is the Renoir of novelists.

The idea that Dickens sentimentalizes children derives from the fame of a few exceptional figures: Oliver (whom he himself defined as an abstraction)[18] and those Sacrificed Innocents, Little Nell, Paul Dombey, and Jo the crossing sweep. In *The Old Curiosity Shop* the Marchioness is much more typical of his children than is Nell, and in *Bleak House* the Jellyby and Pardiggle children more typical than Jo. David Copperfield and his friend Traddles, Philip Pirrip and his friend Pocket, are satisfactory as youths, but as children they are superb. David is not immune from the toadying-bullying malady infecting the boarding-school boys at Salem House. "Mr. Creakle," he tells us (1, 7), "cuts a joke before he beats [his victim], and we laugh at it—miserable little dogs, we laugh, with our visages white as ashes, and our hearts sinking in our boots." When told of his mother's death (1, 9), he is heart-broken, but he is also aware of the "dignity" his bereavement confers upon him and, when the eyes of the other boys were directed his way, he "looked more melancholy, and walked slower." Traddles is the bruised flower among these weeds. A chronic under-achiever, he needs some kind of success and finds it in drawing skeletons (1, 7), which "were easy and didn't want any features." Isolated by his invincible decency as he alone stands up for poor Mr. Mell, he finds

---

[18]Defined in the author's preface as "the principle of Good."

consolation in another slateful of skeletons. A single action can make a Dickens child memorable—for instance the mincing gentility of Trabb's boy as he mocks Pip's great expectations (1, 30): "Don't know yah, don't know yah. 'pon my soul don't know yah!" The diversity of these small characters is remarkable: they range in kind from Master Harry Walmers of *The Holly Tree,* that perfect gentle knight of seven years of age, to the wolf boy of *The Haunted Man,* the waif who, unlike Jo, has been completely brutalized by want and neglect. In the latter story also appear John Tetterby and his fat baby brother, Little Moloch—the sole memorial I know of to a class of martyrs found all over the world; young children with still younger ones fastened in their arms or locked on their backs.

The talent perfected earliest by both Shakespeare and Dickens and exercised most consistently was the ability to create comic characters. Falstaff and Pickwick, during the life of these writers, cast their substantial shadows over all the rest of their progeny. Shakespeare's official jesters have not worn well—we laugh at their jokes in courtesy—but his jests in human shape continue to be irresistible. A few—Falstaff, Juliet's Nurse, Polonius—are important in the action, but the majority are given us as a casual bonus: Cade's rebels, Lance and his dog, Holofernes and Nathaniel, Bottom and company, Touchstone's Audrey, Mistress Quickly, Ensign Pistol, Justice Shallow, Master Slender, the Gravediggers of Elsinore, Dogberry and Verges, Pompey and Elbow, the country victims of Autolycus, Stephano the drunken butler. Attempts to define humor are fatal, but I shall risk pointing to one trait which all these characters share in common: complete faith in their own importance despite massive evidence to the contrary. Since it is a trait we all share, a touch of nature making the whole world kin, our laughter is perforce sympathetic. The comic defect of all stems, not from pure conceit, but from worn-out or untrained minds and from occupational bias, and can no more be submitted to satirical scorn than can simplicity, old age, or calloused hands. Whom after all are we laughing at when old Justice Shallow says, "Certain, 'tis certain, very sure, very sure. Death, as the Psalmist saith, is certain to all, all shall die. How a good yoke of bullocks at Stamford fair?"[19] The rest of us elders have been known to turn our eyes now and then from the words of the Psalmist to glance at the stock-market quotations.

Important roles are played also by some of Dickens's comic characters—Pickwick, Pecksniff, Micawber—but most of them are also in a technical sense minor: Sam Weller's parents and Mr. Stiggens, Sergeant Buzfuz, Beadle Bumble, Dick Swiveller, Wackford Squeers, Crummles and company, Chadband, Melchisedech Howler, Podsnap, Sarah Gamp, Cousin Feenix, Mr. Vholes, Silas Wegg, Pumblechook—the list could be extended indefinitely. In fact, more such characters appear in just two of Dickens's novels, *Martin Chuzzlewit* and *Bleak House,* than in all of Shakespeare's plays. Many are as memorable as Shakespeare's, and amuse us in the same way, evoking laughter which is sympathetic, or at least not hostile. The traits of Juliet's Nurse and Mistress Quickly reappear in Mrs. Crupp of *Copperfield* and bloom to perfection in Sarah Gamp of *Martin Chuzzlewit.* This ministering angel to the ill and washer of the dead (often, not surprisingly, her late patients) is a loquacious, self-indulgent, morally boneless epitome of sleaziness, but so eloquent about her compassionate heart and her respectability (as attested by the invisible Mrs. 'Arris) that we greet each of her appearances with joy. George Meredith was indignant

---

[19] *2 Henry IV* (3, 1).

when Sarah Gamp was matched with Juliet's Nurse,[20] but she is truly just as funny and we get her in larger portions. The comic characters of Dickens are more often villainous than Shakespeare's, but villainous in a stimulating way. Committed to the work ethic, they strive as hard in doing bad as anyone could in doing good. Silas Wegg wears himself so thin in trying to cheat his benefactor Boffin that his wooden leg begins to look positively "chubby."[21] Like Shakespeare, Dickens punishes his villains but refrains from crushing their spirits, unless they are guilty of murder. His comic villains are especially resilient, and we often catch a parting glimpse of them grazing villainously in pastures new.

When his Edwardian detractors treated Dickens as a journeyman caricaturist, they were aware that he deals with surfaces, but unaware that he does so consciously and with consummate artistry. Even the least aggressive of them, the novelist E. M. Forster, wrote with airy patronage of Mr. and Mrs. Micawber as if they were cartoons with bubbles issuing from their mouths, his saying that he is expecting something "to turn up," hers saying she "will never desert Mr. Micawber."[22] There have been periods when Shakespeare's Shylock and Falstaff were similarly seen as cartoons. The latter was portrayed by the eighteenth-century actors as a mere farcical buffoon groveling in fear on the stage. In protest Maurice Morgann wrote the first analysis of a Shakespearean character worthy of its subject: *An Essay on the Dramatic Character of Sir John Falstaff* (1777). Its equivalent could be written on the dramatic character of Wilkins Micawber. In fact, a critic who put his mind to it could prove that Wilkins is as complex and enigmatic as Hamlet.

---

[20]*Letters of George Meredith*, ed. by his son (2v., New York, 1912) 1: p. 206.
[21]*Our Mutual Friend* (3, 14).
[22]E. M. Forster, *Aspects of the Novel* (London, 1927), pp. 93-99.

Let me conclude with a sketch of the bounteous materials Dickens has supplied. Mr. Micawber is introduced (1, 11) as a stout man with an "extensive" face and bald head, dressed in shabby brown surtout and black tights, but sporting an elegant expanse of white collar, a tasseled cane, and an ornamental quizzing-glass or monocle. He speaks in a "rolling" voice and does a great deal of humming—we are not sure whether in happiness that no creditor is at present in sight, or in nervous apprehension that one is about to appear. He confronts us at once with mysteries. Although he and his frayed wife are middle-aged, the eldest of their children is only four, and the youngest, twins, are still nursing—so assiduously in fact that one "hardly ever" saw both "detached from Mrs. Micawber at the same time." Although he has never been, so far as we hear, more than a door-to-door salesman (the rumor that he was once a marine must surely be false) he is earnest, aspiring, educated, and, according to Mrs. Micawber, a man of talent amounting almost to genius. He is genteel to a fault, but no snob; fond of the table, but no cadger of meals; indeed he constantly invites guests home to dinner when the tableware is not in pawn. He is viewed by the tradesmen who stalk him as a complete dead-beat, yet seems, nay *is,* the soul of domestic rectitude. Little David trusts him on sight, and the trust is never betrayed.

Mrs. Micawber's belief in her husband's great gifts is not without foundation. His is the most distinguished conversational and epistolary style ever possessed by a complete failure. He refers to the few shillings he earns as his "pecuniary emolument," and to the dim lodging of his family as their "domiciliary accommodation" (2, 20). His bachelorhood was that time when he was "in a state of celibacy," and Mrs. Micawber "had not yet been solicited to plight her faith at the

Hymeneal altar" (2, 9). He has the Shakespearean knack of saying things in Latinate polysyllables and then translating them into Germanic monosyllables: "The twins no longer derive their sustenance from Nature's founts—in short . . . they are weaned" (1, 17); "I am at present, my dear Copperfield, engaged in the sale of corn upon commission. It is not an avocation of a remunerative description—in other words, it does *not* pay" (2, 8). But sometimes he cannot resist the temptation to follow elegance with elegance: "Mrs. Micawber is in a state of health which renders it not wholly improbable that an addition may be ultimately made to those pledges of affection which—in short, to the infantine group" (2, 8). The brief against Heep which he reads (3, 8) is one of the great documents of accusation. One paragraph is enriched by Shakespearean allusions:

> "Then it was that I began, if I may so Shakespearianly express myself, to dwindle, peak, and pine. I found that my services were constantly called into requisition for the falsification of business, and the mystification of an individual whom I shall designate as Mr. W. . . . This was bad enough; but as the philosophic Dane observes, with that unusual applicability which distinguishes the illustrious ornament of the Elizabethan Era, worse remains behind!"
>
> Mr. Micawber was so very much struck by this happy rounding off with a quotation, that he indulged himself, and us, with a second reading of the sentence under pretense of having lost his place.

That there is a histrionic touch in the Micawber make-up cannot be flatly denied. But its presence frees him from the suspicion that in him as in other geniuses great wit to madness is allied. He is *not* a manic depressive. True, he often weeps, threatens to cut his own throat, and pictures his family dying of "inanition"—first the new babe, then the twins, then the rest in order of their frailty (3, 13)—but he really enjoys these moments of despair as much as the elation which always follows. As Falstaff loves to play Falstaff, so Micawber loves to play Micawber, and his woes give him a chance to compose for himself some magnificent lines. (Perhaps Hamlet himself shows a trace of this propensity.) And Micawber is *not* a megalomaniac. Although often stirred by thoughts of approaching grandeur, he never imagines himself a Napoleon, Don Juan, or anyone else off the ladder he is actuallly trying to climb. With his foot groping for the first rung, he pictures himself at the top, but it is always the top of the right ladder. When he advertises for work with a business firm, he at once sees the family home rising among those of the merchant princes on Oxford Street, and when he begins to serve as clerk for lawyer Heep, he at once sees himself as qualifying for the bar and becoming Lord Chancellor. (His bald head, he reflects practically, will be a convenience in donning the judicial wig.) At the prospect of emigrating to Australia he dresses as a frontiersman, and before he has embarked, he walks with a nautical roll. Morgann set out to prove that Falstaff was not really a coward at all. It could easily be proved that Micawber was not unreliable. He never defaults on a loan that he has not intended to pay; and not even the making of punch gives him so much satisfaction as affixing the government stamps to a new promissory note. The only time he is consciously involved in misdoing (in the office of Heep) he is so lacerated by feelings of guilt that he returns (3, 10) to the scene of his innocent days in debtors' prison, and gazes up at the spikes on the walls "as if they were the interlacing boughs of trees that had shaded him in his youth."

I must cease, although I have scarcely scratched the surface. I have said nothing of this character's arcane relations with his wife, her deceased "mamma and papa," and her often-mentioned but unseen "family." I cannot resist adding a few words about the latter because I can offer a discovery of my own as well as an opportunity for Freudian speculation to any qualified person who wishes to follow the matter up. Why does Mrs. Micawber keep saying that she will never leave Mr. Micawber when she evidently has no place to go? And why does he, who is one of the few characters in Dickens who has no family of his own, so much resent his wife's? He even resists bidding her relations farewell when he takes his flock to Australia (3, 15), on the excuse that they will only respond with "a parting shove of their cold shoulders." The answer to these questions is this. Her relations, fearing that the Micawber children will one day become a burden on themselves, have suggested a separation until the wife is past childbearing age. They have had the effrontery, the callousness, the *indelicacy* to try to get Micawber out of Mrs. Micawber's bed! Chapter and verse will be found in my notes.[23]

Perhaps I have exaggerated a little the infinite variety of this friend of Copperfield's youth—or was it the other way around? His complexity may not be as challenging as Hamlet's, but his creation was no simple matter: we should never patronize the creations of the great. Let me conclude by quoting the ending of Morgann's essay on Falstaff,[24] only substituting a few names:

---

[23] After telling David of his wife's pregnancy (2, 8), Mr. Micawber says: "Mrs. Micawber's family have been so good as to express their dissatisfaction at this state of things. I have merely to observe, that I am not aware it is any business of theirs, and I repel that exhibition of feeling with scorn and with defiance!" At a later date Mrs. Micawber tells David (2, 17) that her family has been informed of the fact that she is resolved to go with her husband when he takes up the duties of his new position in Canterbury: "I may auger, from the silence of my family, that they object to the resolve I have taken." Need more be said? A domestic controversy of long standing, but hitherto concealed from the reader, has momentarily surfaced! It may be added, incidentally, that one of the wonders of the portrayal of this couple is the way the wife's manner of speaking becomes increasingly like her husband's, but remains at the feminine level, never quite achieving the true Micawber grandeur.

[24] Maurice Morgann, *On the Dramatic Character of Sir John Falstaff* [1777], ed. D. N. Smith, *Eighteenth Century Essays on Shakespeare* (Glasgow, 1903), p. 299. (Morgann lists Macbeth, Othello, Benedick, and Falstaff.)

If any one thinks these observations are the effect of too much refinement, and that there was in truth more of chance in the case than of management or design, let him try his own luck—perhaps he may draw out of the wheel of fortune a Sam Weller, a Seth Pecksniff, a William Dorrit, a Philip Pirrip, a Sarah Gamp, or a Mr. Wilkins Micawber.

III. The Welcome Message

1

WE CANNOT say that a play or novel must be morally satisfying in order to be a work of art, but we cannot say either that such satisfaction plays no part in its success. Horace was speaking not in theoretic but in practical terms (the publisher's profit and the author's fame) when he said that poetry must be useful as well as delightful if it is to "cross the seas." It has long since gone out of fashion to speak of the "message" of a work of literary art, but the search for messages continues. The bulk of literary criticism, although written by those presumably most interested in artistic form, still consists of moral evaluation. Even when the critic is engaged, with a show of detachment, in analyzing the author's psychology, or reckoning up his literary indebtedness, it is often easy to see that he is responding to a message he has received, or thinks he has received, from the work under review.

My own preference is for the kind of critic who makes no attempt to conceal his moral concern. Two famous essays written within a year of each other,[1] George Orwell's "Charles Dickens" and Edmund Wilson's "Dickens: The Two Scrooges," have virtues of a contrasting kind. The first is infected by the patronizing tone of the early twentieth-century intellectuals, but Orwell is as honest as Doctor Johnson about his own moral standards, and he tells what he sees in Dickens whether he likes it or not. The effect is good because, in his overall view, Orwell likes what he sees and

---

[1] "Charles Dickens," *Inside the Whale* (London, 1940); "Dickens: The Two Scrooges," *The Wound and the Bow* (Boston, 1941).

convinces us that it is really there. Wilson's essay is more deferential and critically acute, but less trust-inspiring in its overall view. It is, in a measure, a propaganda piece, assuring us that Dickens is our "contemporary," as similar but less skillful depth probes have assured us that Shakespeare is our contemporary. Actually they are not our contemporaries, either in fact or in the sense that they anticipated peculiarly modern attitudes. If their works remain morally relevant, it is not because they are of *our* age but are, "for all time," in which case to modernize is to trivialize them.

One of the best things about recent criticism of Dickens at its best is its insistence that he, like Shakespeare and all great writers, was a conscious artist. To me this means that he knew what he was doing: that the moral thrust as well as the technique of his writing was the product of a superior critical intelligence exercising powers of choice. If some aspect of his message now seems to us unwelcome, obsolete, or even unintelligible, we should not rewrite it, excuse it, or avert our eyes, but look at it very steadily—that is, if we are to understand why it has seemed intelligible and welcome in other times and places. For this reason I shall meet head on the issue presented by his ideal of womanhood and of virtuous sexual conduct. In nearly all the novels appears a female character who serves as a symbol of moral perfection. The symbol achieves highest magnitude and intensity in *Little Dorrit,* there figuring as titular character and focal point of the action. John Wain describes this character as

> . . . a girl who has put all her energies into relieving the sufferings of her weak and selfish father, and as a result is left in a permanently disabled psychological state, in which the relationship of father and daughter is the only one she can think of as real.[2]

---

[2]"Little Dorrit," *Dickens and the Twentieth Century,* ed. J. Gross & G. Pearson (London, 1962), p. 176.

What we have here is a statement of ethical disapproval disguised as psychological analysis. When Wain says that this girl whom Dickens presents as a spiritual paragon is really a spiritual cripple, the critic is saying that the artist did not know what he was doing. Compare his remarks with Lionel Trilling's:

> And we do not reject, despite our inevitable first impulse to do so, the character of Little Dorrit herself. Her untinctured goodness does not appall us or make us misdoubt her, as we expected it to do. This novel is only incidentally realistic; its finest power of imagination appears in the great general images whose abstractness is their actuality . . . and in such a context we understand Little Dorrit to be the Beatrice of the *Comedy*, the Paraclete in female form.[3]

This is precisely right; the critic knows what he and the artist are doing. Yet oddly enough Trilling's words are even more indicative than Wain's of the unwelcome nature of the message conveyed by this symbolic character. Although true and climactically placed, only a few sentences are devoted to her in an essay on a novel she dominates and names. The rest of the essay, like Wain's, is on the novel as social criticism. The sentences themselves are apologetic, assuming that the reader will "reject" little Dorrit, "misdoubt" her, be appalled by her "untinctured goodness." And finally Trilling deploys all that deftness and tact which have made his criticism so persuasive. With a sense that we are broadening our cultural horizons, we hear that Little Dorrit is a "Beatrice," a "Paraclete in female form."

In terms less engaging but still native to the tradition in which Dickens wrote, Amy Dorrit projects the image of the virgin mother. The image first appears in his second novel, *Oliver Twist* (1, 29) in the person of Rose Maylie:

> The younger lady was in the lovely bloom and springtime of

---

[3]Preface to *Little Dorrit* [1953], *Dickens: A Collection of Critical Essays* (Englewood Cliffs, N.J., 1967), p. 157.

womanhood; at that age, when, if ever angels be for God's good purposes enthroned in mortal forms, they may be, without impiety, supposed to abide in such as hers.

She was not past seventeen. Cast in so slight and exquisite a mold; so mild and gentle; so pure and beautiful; that earth seemed not her element.

Nevertheless (and I shall spare you more) this divinity was made for motherhood—"for Home, and fireside peace, and happiness." When he was writing *Oliver Twist,* but before Rose Maylie had appeared in it, Dickens's sister-in-law Mary Hogarth died in his arms. He composed the inscription for her tombstone: "Young, Beautiful, and Good, God in his Mercy numbered Her with His Angels at the Early Age of Seventeen." For years her image haunted his dreams. He wrote to Forster from America, "I feel, in the best aspects of this welcome, some of the presence and influence of that spirit which directs my life, and through a heavy sorrow has pointed upward with unwavering finger for more than four years past."[4] Two years later he wrote from Italy of a half-waking vision in which she appeared to him in blue drapery "as the Madonna might in a picture by Raphael."[5]

It is tempting to trace the Madonna image in Dickens to his devotion to Mary Hogarth (a Protestant's Mariolatry), but this would be a *post hoc propter hoc* error, like tracing the bent of his genius to his boyhood drudgery in a blacking warehouse. What we have really to account for is his devotion to Mary Hogarth in the first place. This must have been the product of her physical attraction and his total past conditioning, including the first stirrings of religious and familial-ethical emotion. The finger pointing upward met his

---
[4]Forster, *Life,* ed. Ley, p. 206.
[5]Letter to Forster, Sept. 30, 1844, *The Letters of Charles Dickens,* ed. Walter Dexter (3 v., London, 1937-1938), **1**: p. 624.

eye in the stained-glass windows of the churches of Chatham and Rochester before he had seen pictures by Raphael. David Copperfield thinks of such windows when he sees Agnes Wickfield (1, 15; 3, 21); and, when Arthur Clennam kneels at the wedding altar with Amy Dorrit (3, 34), sun rays shine upon them "through the painted figure of Our Savior on the window." The maternal quality of these "Paracletes" is as conspicuous as their purity. The defective waif Maggy knows Amy Dorrit as "Little mother." Amy mothers not only Maggy and her weak father, but also her wayward brother and sister, and is prepared to mother her sister's neglected children and her own future husband. Madeline Bray, Agnes Wickfield, and Ethel Dombey mother their distressed fathers. Esther Summerson mothers any child within reach, and of course she and all the rest are destined to mother their own. The list of immaculate women in Dickens, ministering to the weak, especially the defenseless young and the bewildered old, could be extended so as to supply over-whelming proof of the dominance of an ideal.

That it was an ideal, and not merely a personal obsession, is shown by the fact that it was served just as consistently by Shakespeare. His heroines mother fewer miscellaneous children because the exigencies of play-casting in his time placed fewer at their disposal, but their propensity is clear enough. They are all very tender, and all very pure. The first typical example is Silvia of *The Two Gentleman of Verona* (4, 2): "Holy, fair, and wise is she"—scarcely the terms in which modern writers praise their heroines. The type reappears often in the later plays and always in the last. Among her other virtues Miranda is motherly—as a child, even to Caliban. One may not think of the virgin mother as a Shakespearean symbol, but actually he is more explicit in evoking it than Dickens. Dickens's contemporaries associated his heroines with Cordelia ministering to the helpless Lear (4, 4):

> O dear father,
> It is thy business that I go about.

Thaisa of *Pericles* and Hermione of *The Winter's Tale* are mothers in present fact, but when reunited with husband and child, the former is serving in the temple of Diana as High Priestess of the Virgins, and the latter stands on a pedestal like a statue of the Virgin Mary while her daughter kneels:

> And do not say 'tis superstition, that
> I kneel and then implore her blessing.

I might go on with this matter, but will end by reminding you that it is a broken image of the virgin mother that breaks Hamlet's heart.

The Freudian explanation of the symbol will be that the purity is a projection of the male child's sexual jealousy, and the tenderness a projection of his sexual need. But this must be at least partly erroneous. It does not account for the fading of the image in modern literature, unless we assume that Freud changed human nature by explaining it, thus ending one era of sensibility and instituting another. The ideal must have served a purpose, and we can guess at what it was. Before man had so thoroughly conquered Nature as to endanger all species but his own, he himself belonged to an endangered species. A child had a limited chance of survival even within a fostering family, scarcely any chance outside of one; and in such conditions the difference between sexual restraint and sexual freedom could present itself as the difference between the fruitfulness of a family and the sterility of a brothel. The image of the virgin mother is hyperbolic, in the way of symbols generally. After all, the idea of motherhood completely divorced from the idea of sexual indulgence is no more "unnatural" than its opposite.

Needless to say the ideal which informs the image does not always evoke it as we read Shakespeare and Dickens. What we normally see is just a pure and tender girl. All the young heroines of both writers are virginal, and, perhaps in consequence, so also are all their young lovers—the latter, says Silvius, "all made of passion, . . . All adoration. . . . All purity."[6] The virginal quality of the girls is often stressed by a Caliban or Boult, a Gride, Quilp, or Uriah Heep slavering in their vicinity, like the monsters at the feet of the angels in medieval statuary. The quality is also stressed by their extreme youth or dainty size. This has suggested to Frank Harris, Shakespeare's "fierce sensuality,"[7] and to Leslie Fiedler that Dickens's instincts were those of a "child rapist."[8] We must regard such conclusions with reserve. However, there is in neither Shakespeare nor Dickens any sign of ascetic aversion to sexuality itself. The "purity" does not cancel the "passion." Shakespeare smiles upon the sexual impulse, and so also does Dickens, as anyone will notice who does not need photographs and a chart. There is no better portrayal of its early blossoming anywhere in literature than we find in *David Copperfield*. From puberty onward David keeps falling in love: "I adore Miss Shepherd. She is a little girl in a spencer, with a round face and curly hair. I touch Miss Shepherd's glove, and feel a thrill go up the right arm of my jacket and come out at my hair"

---

[6]*As You Like It* (5, 2). Compare the combined passion and "purity of heart" of David's devotion to Dora, *David Copperfield* (2, 7) and the psychological as well as artistic wreckage achieved in the modern attempt of "realistic" revision.

[7]Frank Harris, *The Man Shakespeare* (New York, 1909).

[8]Quoted by Ada Nisbet in *Victorian Fiction, A Guide to Research*, ed. L. Johnson (Harvard Univ. Press, 1964), p. 92.

(1, 18). But the impulse must be subjected to nature's plan. The young couples of both writers are eager to marry and have children. Near the end of *As You Like It* (5, 4) appears a hymn:

> Wedding is great Juno's crown,
> O blessed bond of board and bed!
> 'Tis hymen peoples every town,
> High wedlock then be honorèd.

One would suppose, that in works so copious and kaleidoscopic as theirs, at least one reference to contraception or abortion would occur, but actually none does. There is no context in which one would fit. Even Charmian of *Anthony and Cleopatra,* who is not the motherly type, says (1, 2), "Let me have a child at fifty." This, too, lacks a modern ring.

Our towns are now abundantly "peopled," and enthusiasm wanes for adding to the number who will pollute our air and water, preempt our parking space, and obstruct our view of the lake. Orwell complains that Dickens wants people to multiply "like a bed of oysters."[9] And it becomes increasingly puzzlesome that a strict code of sexual morality, which, in spite of his fondness for ribald jokes, Shakespeare applies even

---

[9] "Charles Dickens" (see note 1), reprinted in *Dickens, Dali, & Others* (New York, 1946), p. 54. Orwell shrewdly but disdainfully pictures the Dickens Utopia as a place where an extended, and extending family live in leisurely comfort and loving companionship. He remarks on its absence of "purpose," without coping with the paradox that such is the defect of every paradise *achieved*. The artistic and intellectual pursuits which Orwell's Utopia would include (and Dickens's does not necessarily exclude) cannot be considered as both ends in themselves and purposeful. Orwell's objection is really academic, since there is small chance that any vision of earthly paradise will become a reality, and the visions themselves do have "purpose." It would be somewhat perverse to read Dickens's vision as advocacy of a population explosion. He was thinking in terms of the present, not of a hypothetical future. His anti-Mathusianism stemmed from his ingrained hostility to viewing human beings in statistical terms with oneself exempted from the calculations. In the third stave of *The Christmas Carol,* Scrooge's reference to the "surplus population" provokes a blank verse rebuke from the accompanying Spirit: "Oh God! to hear the Insect on the leaf pronouncing on the too much life among his hungry brethren. . . !" It can be demonstrated that his sentiment was improvident but not that it was frivolous: the idea of what constitutes the "surplus" might well expand in ratio to the contraction of such sentiment.

more stringently than Dickens, and, like him, to both sexes alike,[10] should have been espoused in defense of life. To see a Dickensian heroine as a procreation symbol may seem as hard as to picture the Vernal Maid clad in a Victorian crinoline, or Venus Genetrix in Salvation Army garb, but millions have had no trouble in reading the code.[11] Dickens viewed celibate sects with an amusing mixture of incredulity and indignation, while Shakespeare paid homage to vestals but rescued his "earthlier" maidens from singing "faint hymns to the cold fruitless moon."[12]

At the opposite pole from the symbol of creation and nurture stands the brutal murderer, symbol of de-

[10] That the Elizabethan was less flexible than the Victorian is signaled in various ways. In Shakespeare the suspicion of adultery inspires tragic scenes of high emotional intensity; in Dickens it inspires grave but low-pitched chapters (such as those involving Doctor Strong and his young wife in *David Copperfield*). In Shakespeare prostitutes are the butt of harsh humor and invective; in Dickens they are viewed compassionately although their fate is pictured as dire. In Shakespeare "bastard" is freely used as a pejorative; in Dickens, when Monks calls Oliver "bastard," Mr. Brownlow sternly rejoins, "The term you use . . . reflects disgrace on no one living but you who use it" (2, 13). The illegitimate Esther Summerson of *Bleak House* represents, like Oliver, "the principle of Good." No evil Edmund figure, returning evil upon his begetter, appears in Dickens although one still does in Walter Scott—the bastard of Sir George Staunton in *The Heart of Midlothian*.

[11] It is now hard to understand the feeling that prompted Landor's statement that Dickens was "with Shakespeare the greatest of English writers, though indeed his women are superior to Shakespeare's" (George H. Ford, *Dickens and his Readers*, Princeton, 1955, p. 57), and Lord Jeffrey's and Leo Tolstoy's opinion that Nell was equal or superior to Cordelia. Dickens' treatment of the death of Nell, as of other children, establishes a religious context and (as we know in the case of Jeffrey) provided what may be called Christian catharsis, but Nell would have been held dear by these men, even if she had survived, because her purity and tenderness qualified her as a mother. That the purity admired in the heroines was not identified as that of vestals is illustrated by Lord Jeffrey's favorite passage in all of Dickens's works (Forster, *Life*, ed. Ley, p. 262). It occurs in *American Notes* (chap. 12) and describes a cheerful and affectionate girl, a sort of frontiers Rosalind, who is approaching her home on a Mississippi steamboat after visiting her sick mother in the East. She has left her husband one month after marriage "in that condition in which ladies who truly love their husbands desire to be" and is now returning with her baby as an offering to him. Dickens in high good humor tells how her joy communicates itself to the other passengers. The success of this offhand sketch makes us realize that one trouble with his heroines is that we see them always in their probationary period, as yet "unfulfilled" He tried, with imperfect success, to mitigate the atmosphere of solemnity by giving some of them the gift of merriment, and in the case of the last three (Estella, Bella Wilfer, Rosa Budd) some humanizing faults.

[12] *Midsummer Night's Dream* (1, 1). Dickens's strictures are not confined to the Catholic orders; see his sketch of a Shaker village in *American Notes* (chap. 15).

struction. The ancient injunction, "Thou shall not kill," retains its emotional validity, but it may do so in part because of works of the imagination. A play like *Macbeth* resorts to subterfuges in order to exercise our feelings of aversion. When we read the chronicles which served as its source, we find that the slaying of Duncan represents an amalgam of several episodes occurring in a lethal dynastic struggle. Among barbaric or semi-barbaric peoples, such episodes are an historical commonplace. A man of prowess wants to occupy a throne and employs the standard means of creating a vacancy. The nucleus of fact had been encrusted with legend and already moralized in the account which Shakespeare read. Nearly everything in his play appears in outline in the chronicle: the supernatural machinery, the instigation by the killer's wife, the fear of detection leading from crime to crime, and the final retribution. The one substantive addition to the story made by the poet is the murderer's own sense of horror at what he does (2, 2):

> Will all great Neptune's ocean wash the blood
> Clean from this hand? No, this my hand will rather
> The multitudinous seas incarnadine,
> Making the green one red.

It is this addition which makes murder in the play seem incomparably more horrible than in the chronicle or in all earlier tragedies of blood. The addition is as irrational as it is effective, violating every historical and psychological probability. The kind of man who is appalled by murder does not commit murder. It is meaningless to say that all men are capable of deadly violence. They well may be, but Macbeth's is no crime of passion but the deliberate slaughter of a friend for gain, an act requiring a moral callousness incompatible with moral sensitivity. The only authenticity which can be claimed for Shakespeare's treatment of murder is its truth to the feelings of non-murderers.

The same thing may be said of Dickens's treatments, as illustrated by the best-known example: Nancy's murder by Bill Sikes. This too has a "source"—not a chronicle, but a journalist's report written by Dickens himself and included in *Sketches by Boz*.[13] An underworld brute is brought for identification to the deathbed of his drab whom he has assaulted. He shows some discomfort at the prospect of being hanged, but remains otherwise surly, stolid, or, as Dickens says, "wholly unmoved." When we compare Dickens's murderer in fact with his murderer in fiction—Sikes wandering about in a daze, haunted by "the dreadful consciousness of his crime" and visions of Nancy's bleeding body—we see that he has done with his killer just what Shakespeare has done with his. He has effected a transplant, giving to a creature who lacked a conscience his own conscience and ours. To recognize this process is to realize the naïveté of the view, occasionally taken in respect to both writers, that persons so successful in portraying murder must have had the capacity to commit it. What they had was capacity to repent it. And Dickens was not inwardly "driven." He knew what he was doing; elsewhere he remarks that ordinary people cannot understand murderers, who operate outside the range of ordinary human feeling. It may at first seem ludicrous to compare the gangster of London with the Thane of Cawdor, but after hearing Dickens read the Sikes episode, the actor Macready, who was the most famous thane of the nineteenth century, stood stunned, muttering in consternation: "Two Macbeths!"[14]

---

[13]"The Hospital Patient." (This source is also "moralized," but by lingering upon the penitence and fidelity of the victim, not the compunction of her murderer.)
[14]Letter to James T. Fields, Feb. 15, 1869, *Letters*, ed. Dexter, **3**: p. 704.

One further point of resemblance in the way these writers present "murder most foul." The killing of Duncan is made to seem catastrophic, sending a shudder through all mankind (1, 7):

>   . . . pity, like a naked new-born babe
> Striding the blast, or heaven's cherubin horsed
> Upon the sightless couriers of the air,
> Shall blow the horrid deed in every eye
> That tears shall drown the wind.

When Sikes takes refuge in Jacob's Island, this nearly deserted slum suddenly fills with people. Hundreds of burning eyes gaze upward at his perch, and a mighty chorus of voices shout curses loud and deep. A mysterious man on horseback appears in the throng shouting, "Twenty guineas to the man who brings a ladder!" It is all surrealistically strange. In the parent event as narrated in *Sketches by Boz* there are no throngs, no enraged voices, no mounted nemesis armed with twenty avenging guineas. There are just two magistrates and a policeman, glumly doing a routine job. Another fancy-girl bashed by another thug—could anything be more boring?

2

We need proceed no further in this direction. Clearly Shakespeare and Dickens transmit messages, sometimes using the same kind of symbolic characters and didactic ruses. The principles they serve are stated explicitly in the decalogue, the sermon on the mount, and other formulations both within and without the Judeo-Christian ethical tradition. Like the approval of chastity and disapproval of murder, the principles are in general life-cherishing. These our major writers differ from most minor writers only in the quality of their partisanship. They do not invent principles but excel in supplying parables.

Many have found it hard to believe that genius can be so specialized, and that a literary genius need not also be a philosophical genius. A man so exceptional must surely have had exceptional ideas. At the very least he must have proceeded from the simple to the complex, helping to codify philosophical systems and to advance programs of collective action. These are "musts" which must be denied. Shakespeare's works have been searched for three centuries, and his system and program remain undiscovered. True he has been shown to be a spokesman for feudalism, but he has also been shown to be a spokesman for the bourgeois forces which dispatched feudalism, and for religious faith and skepticism, hedonism and stoicism, Catholicism and Protestantism, absolute monarchy and constitutional monarchy, and so on. The search continues and he has lately been revealed as an existentialist who was also a romantic nihilist. Only open territory could accommodate systems so numerous and diverse.

Those who extract doctrines from Shakespeare are sometimes name-droppers stealing a testimonial for a doctrine they wish to sell, but more often they really see what they say they do. His works are ingratiating. It is impossible to read them without feeling that their author was an agreeable man, and what is an agreeable man, after all, if not a man who agrees with us? The human solicitude breathing in his pages comes through to the party-man, who feels that it must embrace his pet views as well as himself, on the he-loves-me-he-must-love-my-dog principle. Moreover he observes, and rightly, that Shakespeare is not on the side of his opponents. If he is anti-establishment, he draws comfort from the faulty establishment figures shown in the histories, tragedies, and Roman plays alike; and if he is pro-establishment, he draws comfort from the faulty rebels shown in the same plays. A plague on both your houses is easily construed as a curse on your house and a blessing on mine. Still it is not quite right to say that the "wonderful philosophic impartiality" attributed to Shakespeare by Coleridge implies neutrality or vacant ground. The systems rushing in to occupy it seem drawn not to a vacuum but to something resembling their original moral breeding-place.

The analogous case of Dickens is striking because he is the least likely of English writers to be credited with "philosophic impartiality." Was he not the great partisan? It is when we ask, partisan of what? that we begin to see the resemblance to Shakespeare. His voice has been identified as the very voice of Victorian England, giving ardent expression to all its social, economic, and political confusions, but it has also been identified as a voice of piercing clarity crying for the destruction of Victorian England. Bernard Shaw and a number of later critics have given him two voices, the acquiescent voice of the earlier novels and the dissident voice of the later novels. His fiction has been described as reactionary and revolutionary, socialistic and capitalistic, as well as other incompatible things, including anarchistic. There was indeed a touch of anarchy in Dickens, as displayed in his hatred of bureaucracies and suspicion of social organizations more complex than the extended family, but so there is in most of us; and those who read militantly destructive doctrine in his works belong to the same fringe as those who read nihilism in Shakespeare. The more common subject of debate is whether his novels foster the idea of reform of the whole social structure or just of particular social institutions. The more pertinent question is whether they foster the idea of social reform at all.

We should distinguish, more than has been done, between Dickens in his role as citizen and in his role as literary artist. His public activities, his private correspondence, and the positions he took as magazine editor reveal him as very much the social critic, activist, and reformer. No English writer has spent more time and energy in support of causes, and his efforts were highly practical. His distaste for bureaucratic red tape did not extend to rejection of systematic procedures. He knew that good engineering, and not just goodness of heart, would be needed if London was to have a decent sewage system. Wherever he went he visited hospitals, workhouses, orphanages, prisons, in the hope that he might find ones even a little better than others, so that he might use them as examples in his magazines. It is natural that critics of his novels should think of programs of institutional reform as they observe his picture of the workhouse in *Oliver Twist*, debtors prison in *David Copperfield*, the Court of Chancery in *Bleak House*, the Civil Service or "Circumlocution Office" in *Little Dorrit*, and of economic, political, and educational abuses in one novel after another, especially since he was quite willing to take credit when reforms occurred, for instance in the supervision of Yorkshire schools after his exposure of Dotheboys Hall in *Nicholas Nickleby*. But our knowledge of Dickens as a man can distort our conception of his artistry. If we happened to know that Shakespeare was in the habit of petitioning Elizabeth to rule without the aid of her Privy Council, we might read *Hamlet* in a different way, construing the portraits of Rosencrantz, Guildenstern, and Polonius as an attack on the Elizabethan civil service; certainly the last of these three seems a prime example of a circumlocutionary officer.

Dickens's endeavors as an artist differ from his endeavors as a citizen. In the novels we find no practical suggestions—on how to re-write and administer the Poor Laws, or the laws of bankruptcy, or of inheritance. He shows the Circumlocution Office to be a sink of nepotism and obstruction, but does not advocate civil-service examinations. He exposes the faults of schools, but never suggests what a good curriculum should consist of or how teachers should be trained and licensed. He exposes jobbery in Parliament, but is silent on the issue of expansion of the franchise. At a time when trade unionism and strikes were viewed as insurrectionary, he is on record as maintaining that workers had as much right to organize as employers, but when he comes to write *Hard Times,* presumably the most reformist of his novels, the union official Slackbridge turns out to be as much of a self-serving fake as the factory-owner Bounderby. The workers are told (2, 4) that they can make tyrannical employers tremble. How? By contributing to the funds and bowing to the edicts of the "United Aggregate Tribunal." Dickens fails not only to indicate how institutions should be reformed, but even how they are presently formed. More hard knowledge of the structure and procedures of Victorian institutions is supplied in one or two novels of Trollope than in all the novels of Dickens. The latter are as uninformative about the specific directions which change might take as are the plays of Shakespeare, written under conditions of strict political censorship.

It is true that the Court of Chancery in *Bleak House* appears to be worse than the Lord Chancellor who presides over it, and that industrial Coketown in *Hard Times* has a horrible identity of its own, but neither is the focus of attention in the story or altered at its end. Dickens does not write about society, its institutions, or their reform. As a citizen he was a liberal, often a confused liberal, but as an artist he was a radical—in the sense that he went consistently to the root of things. His novels are not about anti-human social structures but about anti-social human beings—callous, greedy, repressive men. They are also about tender, generous, emancipating men, who move in the same society as the others. Those who follow the dramatic line that Dickens began as one kind of novelist and ended as another tend to ignore inconvenient details. It is true that the redeeming establishment figures, charitable merchant, just lawyer, dedicated teacher, efficient public officer, fail to appear in *Hard Times,* but they reappear in the novels following it. The difference between the earlier and later novels of Dickens, as between the earlier and later plays of Shakespeare is that they are more serious and better written.

3

"The truth is," says Orwell, "that Dickens' criticism of society is almost exclusively moral. . . . His whole 'message' is one that at first glance looks like an enormous platitude: if men would behave decently, the world would be decent."[15] Orwell's way of elevating this "message" into more than a platitude is to consider its negative aspect, whereupon, oddly enough, it becomes political rather than purely moral. The world will not be decent unless men behave decently no matter what institutional reforms or social revolutions occur—to or from capitalism, socialism, communism, or whatever. The most dilapidated system with men of good will in power will work better than the most up-to-date system with self-seeking or stupid men in power. With the main bearing of this conclusion I agree, but I cannot help observing that Orwell proceeds to identify the men of good will as old-fashioned "liberals"—party men after all. I prefer the statement of the message in its positive if more platitudinous form. In his picture of Slackbridge in *Hard Times* Dickens is not attacking labor unions but providing a warn-

---

[15]"Charles Dickens," *Dickens, Dali, & Others,* pp. 5-6.

ing that the wrong kind of labor leader may prove just as exploitive as the wrong kind of employer. The issue is not of organized or unorganized labor but, as always, of moral right and wrong. Neither he nor Shakespeare, despite their occasional mockery of rebels and reformers, come out against systems, parties, causes as such, against the application of new methods of control to new situations. They are simply not concerned with such things. They were aware of what art can accomplish and where their own competence lay.

We are rendering these writers no service when we force upon them a role which they themselves wisely refused to assume. Between Shakespeare's time and ours have appeared the works of such Englishmen as Hobbes, Locke, Newton, Shaftesbury, Mandeville, Hume, Bentham, Godwin, Malthus, Lyell, Mill, Spencer, and Darwin, not to speak of those offered haven in English-speaking lands, Marx, Freud, and Einstein. His message would have to be complex indeed to compete with the facts, theories, and suggested programs offered in these works. So far as Dickens is concerned, although nearly all were available to him they might just as well not have been. George Henry Lewes, whose vocation it was to expound modern philosophical, scientific, and social ideas said that Dickens's novels contained none whatever, and attributed the fact to his deficient education.[16] But if Dickens was deficiently educated in the works of the Enlightenment and later, so also of necessity was Shakespeare. What Shakespeare had to do, and what Dickens did, was to rely upon personal experience and the formulations of racial experience which we call traditional wisdom.

I have said that the life of the mind in families such as those into which they were born was much the same

---

[16] "Dickens in Relation to Criticism," *The Dickens Critics*, ed. Ford & Lane.

even though more than two centuries had intervened. Both were brought up on the same Bible, the same Book of Common Prayer, and the same kind of moral fables and maxims inherited from the Hebraic, Hellenic, Germanic past. This common heritage gives their work a common ethical cast, and a number of shared metaphors; but their works are secular, never expounding and rarely expressing sectarian religious doctrine. Certain religious attitudes are subsumed, primarily humility and reverence, willing recognition of human limitation and mortality, and of an ultimate mystery to which the creation and order of the universe, and the reality of good and evil, must be referred. The presence of these attitudes in the absence of any evidence of firm commitment to particular articles of religious belief has proved puzzling, and even irritating, to some analysts, who are inclined to view the attitudes as slipshod—or illusory, like fruit without a tree. Shakespeare, these say, has no religion, or at least none but a residual sort of Christianity.[17] His philosophy amounts to no more than a sentiment, a feeling. Dickens is wide open to the same charge—that his philosophy amounts to no more than a sentiment, a feeling.

Those who insist upon the political nature of Dickens's novels may be impelled in part by the generous impulse to give them an intellectual status equal to the quality of their artistry. Such status has sometimes been conferred on Shakespeare's plays by insistence upon their scientific accuracy: they have survived the Enlightenment because human nature does not change and they provide expert studies of human nature. This is dubious ground. Shakespeare was a fine observer, but he cannot be certified as a psychologist because his

---

[17]See George Santayana, "The Absence of Religion in Shakespeare," *Interpretations of Poetry and Religion* (New York, 1936); Benedetto Croce, *Ariosto, Shakespeare, and Corneille,* trans. D. Ainslie (London, 1921).

observation of human nature was neither clinically controlled nor objectively reported. I have pointed out that Macbeth's bloody deed seems unnatural to moral people, but his feeling about it natural. To members of Murder Incorporated his deed would seem natural but his feeling about it unnatural. They would view him as a freak, a "pigeon" who mistook himself for a "soldier." All kinds of feeling are natural, in the sense that they occur in nature, and it is conceivable that the works of an author might provide a complete and accurately illustrated catalog, but Shakespeare's do not function in this way: What he and Dickens excel in doing is juxtaposing different kinds of feeling in the interest, not of definition but evaluation, stressing the distinction between the useful and useless kind.

I think we must acknowledge that the message of Shakespeare and Dickens was not dictated in any definable way by any body of theological dogma, philosophic dialectic, scientific fact, or political doctrine. It was a feeling they possessed and communicated. To me this seems no occasion for apology. I speak under the auspices of the American Philosophical Society for Promoting Useful Knowledge. Since there is no such thing as *useless* knowledge, so far as ultimate possibility of practical application is concerned, the title sounds somewhat quaint, but it may serve as a reminder that knowledge, like any other kind of power, must be supplemented by useful feeling if its advancement is to continue to serve "the glory of the creator and the relief of man's estate." The moral issue is inescapable. The more successfully knowledge is promoted, the more we must trust in the success of that cooperating organization of which Shakespeare and Dickens were such eminent members: the society for the promotion of useful feeling.

They proved equal to their task because of the mode

of their promotion. No one who has ever spent more than a few hours with either of them (except under duress) has had to be told that creation is better than destruction, nurture better than neglect, generosity than greed, love than hate, kindness than cruelty, and so on. Advocacy of the obvious begets apathy or even hostility. What people want is not to hear about good feeling but to feel it. Orwell spells out the message of Dickens as "decency." It is a good word, and one that our age, which fears sentiment, can use with a sense of security, but the more descriptive word is *kindness*. Of all the plays and novels in English, those of Shakespeare and Dickens are the kindest. They are the thing they promote. The Elizabethans passed on to succeeding generations their "gentle" Shakespeare. During the Restoration period Dryden said that he admired Jonson but "loved" Shakespeare, and that Fletcher had the softer but Shakespeare the "kinder" soul,[18] the implication being not that he teaches good feeling but that he engenders it. At its very inception the Shakespeare-Dickens analogy was suggested to critics by the three gifts they shared, their powers of imagination, their humor, and their kindness. Tolstoy had his own explanation of what makes an author cross the seas—"the love with which he treats his characters." "That is why," said he, "Dickens' characters are a bond of union between man in America and man in Petersburg."[19] When Dickens died, the nation he had scolded for thirty-five years went into national mourning, now remembering only what Jerrold called "the well of kindness in him."[20] In that brief later period when it was the critical fashion to call his writing childish and vul-

---

[18]John Dryden, *Of Dramatick Poesie* (1668); *Grounds of Criticism in Tragedy* (1679).
[19]Maude Aylmer, *The Life of Tolstoy* (Oxford, 1929) 1: p. 177. (It is hard to reconcile Tolstoy's love of Dickens with his distaste for Shakespeare. The most obvious explanation is that his English was not up to the task of penetrating the latter's idiom.)
[20]Blanchard Jerrold, "In Memoriam," *Gentleman's Magazine,* July, 1870: p. 228.

gar, no one dared to call him a humbug. Indeed it was in the midst of this period that Santayana distinguished him from the kind of moralists who "do not wish mankind to be happy in its own way but theirs," and said, "Love of the good of others shines in every page of Dickens with a truly celestial splendour."[21]

I realize that as I have progressed, the distinction between what these poets did and how they did it, between the pleasure they afforded and the profit, the art and morality, the medium and message, has become increasingly blurred. Perhaps this is as it should be. When unique creative talents and enormous creative energy are so simply and serviceably deployed, to open wider the portals to human enjoyment and to increase the stock of human kindness, the making of art becomes itself a moral act. I hope I have left in no doubt why their message was widely welcomed. We welcome what we need—good tidings—not that human kindness is an estimable thing, but that it is a true, a present, a potent thing. We welcome occasion to hope.

It would be most inappropriate if, after spending three evenings with my audience and these writers, I should end on a note of despair. At the moment it would not appear that a feeling of kindness is the kindling power in the creations of our most talented writers. At the moment there is no playwright or novelist who serves as common bond among us, to whom people of widely varying social and educational backgrounds can turn year after year in happy expectation, knowing that they will be conducted into a world of wonderful words, absorbing events, fascinating people, good fun, and restorative human warmth. However, we wish there were, and that is a good omen. Seasons change, and we should not mistake each wintry one for the beginning of an ice age. Writers like

---

[21]"Dickens" [1920], *The Dickens Critics*, ed. Ford & Lane, p. 149.

Shakespeare and Dickens do not appear in every generation or even every century. The one appeared 248 years after the other, and if a third appears in the year 2060 he will still be on schedule. It may seem a long time to wait, but perhaps this time there will be an earlier spring. In any case we can always anticipate it by returning to Shakespeare and Dickens. We can always get in out of the cold.

Index

Adams, Charles F., 6n
All the Year Round, see Dickens
L'Allegro, see Milton
American Notes, see Dickens
Antony and Cleopatra, see Shakespeare
Appleton, Thomas G., 6
Arabian Nights Entertainments, The, 26, 33n
As You Like It, see Shakespeare
Austen, Jane, 28
Aylmer, Maude, 71n

Barrow, Edward, 10
Beaumont, Francis, 18
Bentham, Jeremy, 68
Bleak House, see Dickens
Bridges, Robert, 15
Britannia theatre, 20-21

Carlyle, Thomas, 22
Chambers, E. K., 18n
Chesterton, G. K., 2
Chimes, see Dickens
Christmas Carol, see Dickens
Coleridge, Samuel Taylor, 64
Condell, Henry, 18, 19
Croce, Benedetto, 69n

Dana, Richard A., 6
Darwin, Charles, 68
David Copperfield, see Dickens
Dexter, Walter, 54n, 61n
Dickens, Charles
　All the Year Round, 21n
　American Notes, 21n; quoted, 59n
　Bleak House, xii, 27, 39, 44, 65, 66; quoted, 33, 37-38; Chadband, 44, Esther Summerson, 55, 59n, Jellyby children, 42, Jo, 42, 43, Pardiggle children, 42, Vholes, 44
　Chimes, The, quoted, 33; Trotty Veck, 26
　Christmas Carol, A, x-xi, 14, 39; quoted, xi, 34, 58n; Marley, 34, Scrooge, x-xii, 26, 27, 34, 39, Spirit of Christmas Present, 25, Tiny Tim, 14

David Copperfield, 2, 35, 65; quoted, 33, 34, 57; Agnes Wickfield, 55, Creakle, 42, Mrs. Crupp, 44, David, 42, 49, 55, 57, Uriah Heep, 33, 35, 47, 57, Littimer, 35, Mr. Mell, 42, Micawber, 7, 8, 36, 44, 45-50, Mrs. Micawber, 45-50, Steerforth, 35, Dr. Strong, 59n, Traddles, 42
Dombey and Son, Cousin Feenix, 44, Esther Dombey, 55, Melchisedech Howler, 44, Paul Dombey, 42
Great Expectations, xii, 27; Estella, 59n, Philip Pirrip, 42, 43, 50, Pocket, 40, Pumblechook, 44, Trabb's boy, 43
Hard Times, 66, 67-68; quoted, 38-39n; Bounderby, 66, Slackbridge, 66, 67
Haunted Man, The, 43; John Tetterby, 43, Little Moloch, 43
Holly Tree, The, 31, Harry Walmers, 43
Little Dorrit, xii, 27, 52-53, 65; quoted, 31, 36; Casby, 31, Arthur Clennam, 35, 36, Mrs. Clennam, 31, Amy Dorrit, 52-53, 55, William Dorrit, 50, Flora Finching, 40, Maggy, 55, Mr. Merdle, 41, Monsieur Rigaud, 31
Martin Chuzzlewit, 26, 44; quoted, 33n; Sarah Gamp, 36, 44-45, 50, 56, Pecksniff, 44, 50, Todgers, 33n
Mrs. Lirriper's Lodgings, quoted, 34-35; Mrs. Lirriper, 36
Mugby Junction, quoted, 35
Mystery of Edwin Drood, The, 27; quoted, 34; Rosa Budd, 59, Canon Crisparkle, 27
Nicholas Nickleby, 14, 65; Madeline Bray, 55, Vincent Crummles, 44, Gride, 57, Mrs. Nickleby, 40, Nicholas, 41, Wackford Squeers, 14, 41, Smike, 1
Old Curiosity Shop, The, xi, 31, 32;

"Marchioness," 1, 42, Little Nell, 1, 59n, Quilp, 31, 32, 57, Dick Swiveller, 1, 6, 44
   Oliver Twist, xii, 1, 13, 27, 65; quoted, 15, 54, 59n, 61, 62; Beadle Bumble, 44, Noah Claypole, 5, Fagin, 13, Rose Maylie, 53-54, Monks, 59n, Nancy, 13, Oliver, 27, 28, 42, 59n, Bill Sikes, 28, 61-62
   Our Mutual Friend, 27; Boffin, 45, John Harmon, 27, Podsnap, 44, Bella Wilfer, 59n, Silas Wegg, 44, 45
   Pickwick Papers, 13, 22; Buzfuz, 44, Mr. Pickwick, 1, 26, 43, 44, Stiggens, 44, Sam Weller, 1, 36, 50, Tony Weller, 44
   Sketches by Boz, 61; quoted, 62
   Somebody's Luggage, quoted, 44
   Tale of Two Cities, A, 27
   Uncommercial Traveller, The, 20; quoted, 21, 21n, 37
Dickens, John, 6, 7, 8, 9
Dickens, William, 5, 9
Dombey and Son, see Dickens
Dramatic Character of Sir John Falstaff, see Morgann
Droeshout engraving, 6
Dryden, John, 71

Einstein, Albert, 68
Elizabeth I, Queen, 65

Felton, Cornelius C., 1-2, 3
Fiedler, Leslie, 57
Fielding, R. J., 12n
Fletcher, John, 71
Ford, George H., 12n, 36n, 68n, 72n
Forster, John, 7, 10, 16, 19, 42, 44, 45
Freud, Sigmund, 56, 68

Gad's Hill Place, 10
Gissing, George, 2, 14, 40n
Gladstone, William, 12
Godwin, William, 68
Goldsmith, Oliver, *The Vicar of Wakefield,* xiii
Great Expectations, see Dickens

Hall, Joseph, *Virgidemiarum,* 15
Hamlet, see Shakespeare
Hard Times, see Dickens
Harris, Frank, 57
Haunted Man, see Dickens
Heart of Midlothian, see Scott

Hemming, John, 18, 19
Henry the Fourth, see Shakespeare
Henry the Fifth, see Shakespeare
Henry the Sixth, see Shakespeare
Hobbes, Thomas, 68
Hogarth, Mary, 54
Hogarth, William, 33n
Holly Tree, see Dickens
Horace, 23, 51
Horne, R. H., 33n, 40n
House, Madeline, 9n, 10n, 11n, 14n
Hume, David, 68
Huxley, Aldous, 3

Jeffrey, Francis, Lord, 2, 59n
Jerrold, Blanchard, 71
Johnson, Edgar, 22n
Jonson, Ben, 8, 25
Joyce, James, 23; *Ulysses,* 40
Julius Caesar, see Shakespeare

Kafka, Franz, 23
King, Lear, see Shakespeare
Kyd, Thomas, *The Spanish Tragedy,* 22

Landor, Walter Savage, 2, 59n
Lane, Lauriat, 36n, 68n, 72n
Lang, Andrew, 12
Lewes, George Henry, 36, 68
Lister, T. H., 33n
Little Dorrit, see Dickens
Locke, John, 68
Longfellow, William Wadsworth, 6
Love's Labor's Lost, see Shakespeare
Lydia Languish (*The Rivals*), 13
Lyell, Sir Charles, 68

Macbeth, see Shakespeare
Maclise, Daniel, 6
Macready, William Charles, 61
Malthus, Thomas Robert, 68
Mandeville, Bernard, 68
Martin Chuzzlewit, see Dickens
Marx, Karl, 68
Masson, David, 2
Measure for Measure, see Shakespeare
Merchant of Venice, see Shakespeare
Meredith, George, 44-45
Merry Wives of Windsor, see Shakespeare
Metamorphoses, see Ovid
Midsummer Night's Dream, see Shakespeare
Mill, John Stuart, 68
Milton, John, *L'Allegro,* 21
Mitford, Mary Russell, 2

INDEX

Morgann, Maurice, *An Essay on the Dramatic Character of Sir John Falstaff*, 45n, 49-50
Mrs. Lirriper's Lodgings, see Dickens
Much Ado About Nothing, see Shakespeare
Mugby Junction, see Dickens
Mystery of Edwin Drood, see Dickens

New Place, 10
Newton, Sir Isaac, 68
Nicholas Nickleby, see Dickens
Nisbet, Ada, 57n
Norton, Mrs. Andrew, 1
Norton, Charles Eliot, 1

Old Curiosity Shop, see Dickens
Oliver Twist, see Dickens
Orwell, George, 51-52, 58, 67, 71
Othello, see Shakespeare
Our Mutual Friend, see Dickens
Ovid, *Metamorphoses*, 25

Payne, Edward F., 6n
Pericles, see Shakespeare
Pickwick Papers, see Dickens
Proust, Marcel, 23

Quincy, Josiah, Jr., 25

Racine, Jean Baptiste, 29
Raphael, 54, 55
Renoir, Pierre, 42
Romeo and Juliet, see Shakespeare
Rowe, Nicholas, 7, 8
Rymer, Thomas, 3

Santayana, George, 69n, 72
Scott, Sir Walter, 13, 20; *The Heart of Midlothian*, 59n
Shaftesbury, Anthony Ashley Cooper, First Earl of, 68
Shakespeare, Henry, 9
Shakespeare, Joan, 9
Shakespeare, John, 5, 7, 8
Shakespeare, Richard, 5
Shakespeare, William,
  Antony and Cleopatra, quoted, 58; Charmian, 58
  As You Like It, xiii; quoted, 57, 58; Audrey, 43, Orlando, 41, Silvius, 57, Touchstone, 43
  Hamlet, 26, 30; quoted, 17, 22, 34; Gravediggers, 15, 43; Guildenstern, 65, Prince Hamlet, 2, 34, 49, 56, Ophelia, 30, Polonius, 43, 65, Rosencrantz, 65, Yorick, 34
Henry the Fourth, King, Part One, quoted, 25, 33; Falstaff, 25, 33, 36, 43, 45, 49, 49n, Mistress Quickly, 43, 44
Henry the Fourth, King, Part Two, quoted, 44; Falstaff, 25, 36, 43, 45, 49 49n, Pistol, 43, Mistress Quickly, 43, 44, Justice Shallow, 43, 44
Henry the Fifth, King, quoted ix, 13; Fluellyn, ix, King Hal, 2, Pistol 43, Mistress Quickly, 43, 44
Henry the Sixth, King, Part Two, 15, 17; Jack Cade, 43
Julius Caesar, 27, 35; Brutus, 2
King Lear, 30, 35; quoted, 27, 56; Cordelia, 56, 59n, Goneril, 35, Oswald, 35
Love's Labor's Lost, 34; Berowne, 34, Holofernes, 43, Nathaniel, 43
Macbeth, 25, 27, 30, 60-61; quoted, 60, 62; Macbeth, 28, 29-30, 70
Measure for Measure, Angelo, 27, Pompey, 43
Merchant of Venice, The, x-xii; 25; quoted, 10, 33; Lorenzo, x, Portia, x, Shylock, x-xii, 36, 39, 45
Merry Wives of Windsor, The, Falstaff, 25, 36, 43, 47, 49, 49n, Pistol, 43, Mistress Quickly, 43, 44, Slender, 43
Midsummer Night's Dream, A, 26, 30; quoted, 32, 33, 59; Bottom, 36, 43, Titania, 50
Much Ado about Nothing, quoted, 10; Benedick, 49n, Dogberry, x, 43, Verges, 43
Othello, 35; quoted, 36; Desdemona, 36, Iago, 35, Othello, 36, 49n
Pericles, Boult, 57, Marina, 28, Thaisa, 56
Romeo and Juliet, 39, quoted, 33, 34; Mercutio, 34, Nurse, 43, 44
Sonnet III, quoted, 2
Taming of the Shrew, The, 26
Tempest, The, 26; quoted, 15; Ariel, 27, Caliban, 55, 57, Miranda, 55, Prospero, 2, 25, 29, Stephano, 43
Two Gentlemen of Verona, The, Lance, 15, 43, Silvia, 55
Winter's Tale, The, 26, 30; quoted, 5, 56; Autolycus, 43, Hermione, 56, Perdita, 27, 30

Shaw, George Bernard, 2, 64
Sidney, Sir Philip, 3
Sir Thomas More, 18
Sketches by Boz, see Dickens
Somebody's Luggage, see Dickens
Sonnet III, see Shakespeare
Southampton, Earl of, 11n
Spanish Tragedy, see Kyd
Spencer, Herbert, 12, 68
Spurgeon, Caroline, 32
Stanley, Lord, later 14th Earl of Derby, 11n
Storey, Graham, 9n, 10n, 11n, 14n
Stowe, Harriet Beecher, *Uncle Tom's Cabin*, 22

Tale of Two Cities, see Dickens
Taming of the Shrew, see Shakespeare
Tempest, The, see Shakespeare
Tolstoy, Leo, 23, 28, 59n, 71
Trilling, Lionel, 53
Trollope, Anthony, 20, 38, 66; *The Way We Live Now*, 41n

Two Gentlemen of Verona, see Shakespeare

Ulysses, see Joyce
Uncle Tom's Cabin, see Stowe
Uncommercial Traveller, see Dickens

Van Ghent, Dorothy, 33n
Verulam, Francis Bacon, Lord, 11n
Vicar of Wakefield, see Goldsmith
Virgidemiarum, see Hall
Voltaire, François, 3

Wagenknecht, E., 1n
Wain, John, 52-53
Way We Live Now, see Trollope
Wilkins, W. G., 25n
Wilson, Edmund, 25, 51-52
Wilson, John Dover, 6n
Winter's Tale, see Shakespeare
Woolf, Virginia, 3

OHIO UNIVERSITY LIBRARY

Please return this book as soon as
finished with it. In order to avoid
be returned by the latest